TOWARD A *PENTECOSTALISTA* THEOLOGY

WOMEN DRIVEN BY THE HOLY SPIRIT

Toward a *Pentecostalista* Theology

Women Driven by the Holy Spirit

Miriam E. Figueroa Aponte

Cherohala Press
Cleveland, Tennessee

Toward a *Pentecostalista* Theology
Women Driven by the Holy Spirit

Published by Cherohala Press
900 Walker ST NE
Cleveland, TN 37311
USA
email: cptpress@pentecostaltheology.org
website: www.cptpress.com

Library of Congress Control Number: 2021942503

ISBN-13: 9781953358158

Scripture quotations are taken from the New King James Version unless otherwise noted.

Galatians 3.27-29

For as many of you as were baptized
into Christ have put on Christ.

There is neither Jew nor Greek, there is neither
slave nor free, there is neither male nor female;
for you are all one in Christ Jesus.

And if you are Christ's, then you are Abraham's seed,
and heirs according to the promise.

2 Corinthians 3.17

Now the Lord is the Spirit;
and where the Spirit of the Lord is, there is liberty.

DEDICATION

To my husband José W. Pimentel,
because you have walked this path with me and have allowed
me to develop to the fullest of my abilities.

To Laura Enid, Carlos Javier, and José Javier,
our children, who have witnessed my struggles.

To my grandchildren
Kalani, Mía, Valeria, Brooklyn, Leon, and Mikaela;
hopefully they will inherit an unbiased church.

CONTENTS

FOREWORD

> To the wind of the Spirit that carried away, at Pentecost, the prejudices, interests, and fear of the apostles and opened the doors of the Upper Room widely, so that the community of Jesus' followers would always be open to the world and free in his word and coherent in his witness and invincible in its hope. To the wind of his Spirit that always takes away the new fears of the church.
>
> – Pedro Casaldáliga

One of the women who have impressed me the most in recent years is Dr. Miriam E. Figueroa-Aponte. I learned to value her when we appointed her president of FIEL IV (International Fraternity of Educators and Leaders for the Church of God) in Teresópolis, Brazil.

Since then, I have been observing her in her personal, ministerial/pastoral, and academic development. On several occasions I have had the opportunity to visit her in La Isla del Encanto, Puerto Rico, a model church where she served as co-pastor with her beloved husband, Pastor José Pimentel. Undoubtedly, Miriam has been shaping the ministerial and academic path for a whole new generation of women who today rise up in an invincible spirit of hope in their commitment to the task of the Kingdom.

Miriam, as we affectionately call her, is a woman who thinks of her faith and her ministry with great responsibility. The coherence and excellent articulation of her thoughts, bathed with life experiences and deep theological-Pentecostal reflection, have a hopeful effect on the new generations of women who today prepare to serve in the Kingdom of God with passion, vision, values, talents, gifts, and competencies. Miriam has found her theological voice that rises strongly and determinedly from a biblical and historical framework to free the Latina and Pentecostal woman in order to match her identity, ministerial function, and leadership with that of the male. In order to grow, we must match, if we cannot see man and woman as holy priesthood, equal before the Lord, we cannot maximize the potential and cannot discover the spiritual capacity of the Church.

Not only were women mission protagonists at the beginning of the Church of the first century, but they have also been strategic instruments that God has used throughout the history of Christianity. This is repeated in the expansion of the Church of God (Cleveland, TN) at the beginning of the last century, when women committed to a clear missionary call brought the gospel message to countries such as Mexico, Brazil, and Chile, to name a few. Today, more than half of the global Latino Church are women committed to mission. Most of our students at institutes and ministerial seminaries are Pentecostal women who claim to have received a clear call from God for a full ministerial service. In all Latin American countries, we have a significant and growing percentage of pastors. It is also nice to note that the most numerous Churches of God in Latin America are shepherded by women ministers.

Towards a Pentecostalista Theology: Women Driven by the Holy Spirit will tell us in a pleasant and entertaining way a strong analysis of women's theologies, a clear Pentecostal Pneumatology, an approach to Pentecostal theology and to the prophetic action of justice as women and men.

It is clear that one of the greatest challenges of Pentecostalism is the issue of gender. According to Elizabeth Salazar-Santana, the gender issue allows us to see a contradiction between the principles of community that are lived among those turned into the community of faith and the practice of an unequal ecclesiastical hierarchy. One of the main ambiguities in this issue is reflected in the tension between community life and the vision of the church as an institution. It is clear that Pentecostal movements recognize that women make their expression of faith in such a way that they break the social order of discrimination. While women participated in the expansion of Pentecostalism by leading clear missionary processes, today they do not occupy the same spaces of equality in Pentecostal communities and structures despite being a majority in church membership.

Dr. Figueroa seeks in this work to reverse the situation of women exposed in contemporary Pentecostalism in order to do justice to the present gender challenge and thus empower Pentecostal Latinas, considering other elements that make them subjects of their own lives. Let us pray then, that the Wind of the Spirit may remove from them the great fears of God's Church.

David E. Ramírez, DMin
Assistant General Overseer of the Church of God

ACKNOWLEDGMENTS

The Center for Latino Studies (CEL) of the Pentecostal Theological Seminary in Cleveland, Tennessee has been instrumental in the production of this book in Spanish. With the support and direction of Dr. Wilmer Estrada-Carrasquillo I was able to finish what I thought would take longer. But this is certainly the time. Thank you, Wilmer!

I also thank Dr. Jesús Rodríguez, my thesis director, because he always believed in me. His support has been fundamental, and he was certainly a facilitator and mentor. I remember his words in defending my work: 'You just nailed your thesis to the gates of the Church of God Mission Board'. Yes, I felt like Luther! God bless you always Dr. Rodriguez!

After publishing in Spanish, I approached CPT Press with the proposal to translate the book into English and make it available to a broader audience both in the Academy and in the Pastoral Ministry. Thus, CPT Press, Dr. Chris Thomas, and Dr. Lee Roy Martin were instrumental producing the book that you have in your hands. Dr. Martin has been especially generous, giving his time and effort to make this edition possible. I really appreciate you, Dr. Lee Roy!

I express much gratitude to the Church of God Mission Board (COG) Ríos de Agua Viva in Aguas Buenas, Puerto Rico. It is the church where my husband and I served as pastors for seventeen years. Thank you for allowing me time, helping me financially, praying for me, and walking this path with me. You are a blessing to our lives!

Furthermore, I thank the Church of God Mission Board of Puerto Rico, where I have served for more than two decades. You have opened the doors for me and tried to understand the struggle I have endured along with a handful of brothers and sisters.

Finally, I must thank my husband, José W. Pimentel (Willy), so much for his emotional maturity, because he knows how to protect me; and he knows how to rejoice in my accomplishments without feeling threatened. Thank you, because you always said you wanted me to develop to the fullest of my capacities. Thank you for understanding my challenges, struggles, and frustrations. I love you!

PREFACE

I am a Pentecostal woman. I was born in the Missionary Church of Christ, a Pentecostal denomination native to Puerto Rico. When I was born, my father Jesus M. Figueroa was already the minister of this church. It was in that church and in our home that I began to form my knowledge about God. In our congregation, the worship service was celebrated with joy; and it was imbued with the power of God. I can describe these meetings as 'parties of the Spirit'.[1] In that church God saved people. People would come to church, and they would give their hearts to the Lord. As new Christians, they then became 'hallelujahs'. 'God continued to add to the church those who were to be saved' (Acts 2.47).

In our congregation, God also baptized with his Holy Spirit. I saw the movement of the Holy Spirit and was astonished when an old woman danced with her eyes closed and skipped over the microphone and guitar wires without getting tangled up in them. I also saw the Lord baptize with his Spirit the teenagers who sought the presence of God. Some spoke in other languages, and I remember wanting the same experience. Now, our congregation did not emphasize speaking in tongues alone; it also taught of the fruit of the Spirit. So, the people who were transformed caused astonishment in their communities and took the opportunity to bring others to church. Those transformed by the power of God were now living letters that told what God could do.

I remember that when I was only a twelve-year-old child, we experienced a powerful move of God in that congregation of between two hundred and three hundred members and that our attendance on Sundays would be up to four hundred

---

[1] Darío López Rodríguez, *La fiesta del Espíritu: espiritualidad y celebración pentecostal* (Ediciones Puma: Lima, Perú, 2006), pp. 25-61.

people. One Sunday night we started singing and could not stop. We sang for quite some time, (some say we were singing about thirty minutes):

> I am happy, I am happy, because Jesus Christ saved me.
> Now I sing joyfully because Christ my soul rescued.
> I cannot go back to my old ways anymore
> Because the world can give me nothing.
> I am happy, I am happy, because Jesus Christ saved me.

Then my dad, the pastor, preached and made the call to the altar. All the guests that were there that night, more than ten, went on to give their hearts to Christ. Among them was a man with cancer in his esophagus who had been diagnosed as incurable and awaited death. That night my dad anointed him with oil, and after three days the man was completely free of that cancer. Over the years he became a trumpeter; and even as I write today, he serves the Lord. He ministers to people with cancer, and he wrote his testimony in a treatise narrating his experience of conversion and healing. I saw so many people powerfully healed in the church. In fact, I also saw God delivering those oppressed by the devil with chains of great affliction, who came to find peace in the midst of their tormented lives.

In our home I learned to appreciate the power of God and his provision for us. My parents were humble. They did not own many material things. The pastoral wage was extremely low, even though my father served as pastor/minister for many years. I do not remember us having medical health insurance, so we would rely many times on God to work healing and to support what was preached. So, I experienced the power of God when he healed my brothers: he healed the ears of my second brother Jesus Jr., and the blistered feet of my third brother, Ruben. God also healed me from rheumatic fever at thirteen. God strengthened my father's health as he went to the leper sanatorium to minister to them God's teaching, and he delivered my mother, Anita, during her risky births when she was anemic. On another occasion when we experienced scarcity, someone came to our house with food miraculously. Ruben, my brother, was filled with the Holy Spirit at an early age; and it was so emotional to see him jump like a lamb. So many miracles, care, testimonies, and so many stories. I am Pentecostal, and I cannot depart from that experience that marked my life.

Precisely, I too was blessed to be filled with the Holy Spirit. That experience I have longed for since my teenage years came in my early adulthood under the ministry of Nicanor Estremera. After preaching, Brother Estremera called to the altar those who wished to be baptized with the Holy Spirit of God. I walked down that aisle and he extended his big hands and just pointed at me. Suddenly I was immersed in that powerful experience. From my inside came all those unintelligible words that I could not stop, even though I placed my hands on my mouth in an attempt to control God's touch over my life. Experiences such as the ones I have narrated from my childhood and youth continue to happen today in different parts of the world; because even today, the miracles, wonders, and signs that accompanied the early church continue to happen.

I am Pentecostal, and I am Hispanic, too. I was born in Puerto Rico, where I lived until I was nineteen. Then, when I got married, I went to live in the state of Pennsylvania in the United States, where my husband, Jose W. Pimentel, had gone to work. I had started my studies in Special Education at the University of Puerto Rico and was able to transfer to Kutztown University to complete them. At that time, in the 1990s, I was the only Puerto Rican to arrive from the island to that college, although there were two other Hispanics raised in the United States. I remember my fears, the discrimination, and my struggle to prove my intelligence while struggling with a second language. It was a difficult but challenging time. My husband, who always believed in my abilities, encouraged, and supported me in every project and every dream that came to my mind. We were in Allentown for five years, and I was able to experience what it is like not to be part of the dominant majority; but I did not use that as an excuse to stop on the road.

I had always enjoyed studying English; and saw the great opportunity to improve it. Therefore, although sometimes I felt frightened, I asked God for courage; and the day came that I graduated with honors with my bachelor's degree in education. There in Pennsylvania, my husband, my first daughter Laura, and I served as members of the Assemblies of God Church in Allentown. I always remained connected to the family of faith, contributing in everything I could as a teacher, youth counselor, and ministering in music.

Church is part of my life. I value my Pentecostal experience, and I am honored to be a Latina. Now I understand that God had held my hand and that this training experience in my life was necessary. It was in ministry and during my academic preparation that I understood that God called me to proclaim in a prophetic voice that God's mission is for all and that the Holy Spirit of God enables women to exercise the gifts they have received.

INTRODUCTION

This work is the product of my thesis for the doctoral program in Practical Pastoral Theology at the Inter-American University of Puerto Rico. When I finished defending the thesis, the members of my committee urged me to write about my work. By that time, I had in mind the chapters of this book that I am writing now, with the intention of raising another voice of a Pentecostal and Hispanic woman both in the theological circles and in the local and institutional ecclesial contexts.

When I started in doctoral work, there were ten students, and I was the only woman. In the group, we were five Pentecostal students, three Protestants, one Catholic, and one charismatic. I had very interesting challenges, but it was definitely a very enriching experience. My voice was heard in that space; I liked to reflect and to share my perspectives with my friends and colleagues. I really enjoyed the learning experience. But I confess that it is very difficult as a married woman, a mother, a pastor of a church, and an Academic Dean to finish a doctoral degree. It took me ten years to complete the courses, the comprehensive examination, the thesis proposal, and finally the thesis. How many times I thought it would not end! How many times I wondered if it was worth all the effort! Who would hear about the conflict that I worried about? Would there be a way to present a solution to this one? How would my church take it, my denomination? Despite the difficulties, God has always placed people in my pathway who would understand that my scholarship is part of the mission of God, who guides my destiny.

Along the way, when talking about the subject, the reactions have been diverse. Many have understood how I want to transform certain elements within our Pentecostal churches. Others have wanted to sit down and ask me questions. I have written to the highest leadership of my church, the Church of God, explaining that this gender difference in the exercise of gifts is no longer acceptable. However, along the way I have also engaged with some brothers and sisters who prefer to turn their backs on us because they believed that women should be anonymous. The point is that here I am, with a great desire that the Pentecostal church that I value so much can realize that the conflict presented here must be resolved for the wellbeing of the church itself and for the fulfillment of the mission of God in the world.

Overview of the Book

Chapter 1 describes the limitations placed on women within the Church of God in the United States and Puerto Rico, a denomination that is framed in a hierarchical structure and is dominated by white males in the southern United States. As part of this ecclesiastical structure, the Puerto Rican church, in this case the Mission Board, although it has shown openness to the ministry of women, has not fully recognized the call of women with gifts received from the Holy Spirit. In addition, I explain the concept of *Pentecostalista* theology.

Chapter 2 introduces the theologies that help us understand the conflict of women's pastoral ministry in the total exercise of gifts. Aspects of Practical Pastoral Theology and its methods are briefly described, including some historical notes. The reader is also introduced to the nature and history of feminist theologies. I explain where I establish bonds and breaks with these feminist theologies; and finally, I apply a new paradigm that can be useful to us to seek a solution to the conflict in question.

In Chapter 3, I discuss the issue of Pentecostal pneumatology. How do Pentecostals understand the Holy Spirit? How could this understanding help us resolve the conflict of the exercise of the gifts of Pentecostal women? Is this understanding part of the solution?

Chapter 4 begins by explaining the task of *Pentecostalista* theology. It then presents my model for resolving the ecclesial conflict experienced by women ministers in the Church of God.

Then in Chapter 5, the hermeneutical method of *Pentecostalista* theology is presented. I correlate it with the method of seeing, judging, and acting of the Ibero-American European practical pastoral theology of Casiano Floristán. This method moves in specific steps: awareness, rereading of the Bible, and acting under the direction of the Holy Spirit.

Chapter 6 describes the interlocutors who are Pentecostal women and men together as prophets of justice. It is not a task that belongs only to women. On the contrary, it must be our male brothers in positions of leadership who initiate actions that will make us partakers of the mission of the body of Christ.

In the final chapter, I offer a conclusion and an invitation to draw near to the Lord, to come to the altar where we can confess our faults.

Finally, this book is intended to reach various audiences, because it is necessary to discuss the subject with each of them. First, it goes to the people who lead in our ecclesiastical structures – including pastors – because they have the power to make decisions. Second, it addresses students in our theological institutions and seminaries who are preparing to lead our congregations. Thirdly, it addresses women with God's call, because they struggle with that call. Some of them think erroneously that God has called them because there are no men fit for the task. Such a perspective is detrimental to all parties. Finally, I address this text to Pentecostals in particular and to other denominations in general, because my contention that women ministers should have the same opportunities as male ministers and be eligible to hold the same positions as male ministers is one of the challenges facing the contemporary church.

I therefore invite you, if you are part of any of these groups, to read this work carefully and to respond by acting under the direction of the Holy Spirit.

1

CONFLICT

> Pentecostals continue to grow today
> in part because they can change.[1]
> – Harvey Cox

The Pentecostal church in which I grew up did not distinguish between the ministry of women and that of men. Both men and women could exercise their gifts in any ministry of the church. My dad came to have women as assistant pastors in his long ministerial career. There were teachers, women and men missionaries, and people of both sexes who shared the leadership of the church.

For my part, I excelled in ministerial tasks within the church from an early age. By the age of twelve, I was dedicated to teaching all the preschoolers at church. So, in that Pentecostal congregation, under the ministry of my parents and the leaders of the church, God trained me, formed me, and separated me. Our family ministered in an independent charismatic church for ten years where we could all exercise our leadership at any level. However, upon joining the Church of God in Puerto Rico (Mission Board), we discovered another reality.

---

[1] Harvey Cox, *Fire from Heaven: The Rise of Pentecostal Spirituality and the Reshaping of Religion in the 21st Century* (London: Cassell, 1996), p. 87.

The church's ministerial or business meetings were the first place where I realized something was different. The women, for the most part, were sitting in the back and not participating in the discussions. There were women pastors from various Mission Board congregations, but they were not involved in the affairs. They were allowed to vote, but their voices were absent in discussing matters concerning churches. Of course, I came from a context where men and women participated in church business meetings, so, I was intrigued. I began to investigate, and I discovered a conflict that I decided to study from the discipline of Practical Pastoral Theology.

In addition to the practices that I was experiencing, I discovered that the denominational policy of the Church of God (COG, Cleveland, TN) in general and the Church of God Mission Board (IDDMB) in particular allows women to exercise positions of pastoral ministry, but only up to the second level of credentials, (according to the COG administrative system) thus limiting the possibility that women will serve at the same level of leadership as male ministers.[2] So, the women of this

---

[2] The COG has chosen titles such as exhorter (first rank), ordained minister (the intermediate rank), and ordained bishop (the highest rank of credentials). On the one hand, the church recognizes that these titles 'have nothing to do with the essential meaning of ordination; that is, they do not arise from biblical language nor are they the product of biblical exegesis. These are the product of a tradition in Church government, but they are not biblical terms' (*Enseñanzas, disciplina y gobierno de la Iglesia de Dios, 72da. Asamblea General Internacional,* 2008, p. 162). On the other hand, ordination is understood as 'the act by which the church confirms God's call upon a minister and sends him by the Holy Spirit.' For its part, the COG understands that it is convenient for the church to require different stages for the demonstration of the calling and the gifts. This demonstration must be evidenced in the life and ministry of the person during his active participation in the ministry of the body of Christ. As for the ranks of credentials and the ministry of women in the COG, the following is a summary statement:

Women ministers shall hold the same ministerial titles as male ministers, with all the requirements, duties and responsibilities and ministerial opportunities enjoyed by male ministers in the first or second rank of ministerial credentials ... It should be understood that women do not qualify for the rank of Ordained Bishop' (*Enseñanzas,* S61. El Ministerio de la Mujer, p. 169.)

Pentecostal church cannot exercise the gifts received from the Holy Spirit in the same way as their male brothers. Although in Puerto Rico (in IDDMB) the church has overcome some of these limitations, these policies are influenced by prejudged ideological constructs against women. This dilemma is not simply structural, but theological and historical; and this limits women in ministry from aspiring to high leadership positions that require the third level of credentials, namely the credentials of Ordained Bishop.

I then set out to examine this conflict from Practical Pastoral Theology and from women's theologies, as they inform the struggles for the liberation of women in our Pentecostal church. In practical and concrete terms, my study calls for women's leadership capabilities to be given equal standing to those of men and for the granting of ministry responsibilities in such a way that women can occupy positions of power and authority within the COG. In addition, since the study was carried out from the tradition of Pentecostal faith, ontological arguments will be presented here that attempt to respond to the theology of the COG in particular and the Pentecostal tradition in general, as a way of resolving the conflict of the Pentecostal women called by God to serve within our congregations.

With this in mind, I set out to develop a theology of the Pentecostal and Hispanic woman of the ministry of the church that was consistent with both the experience of women pastors and women with other gifts and with the church's understanding of its pneumatology. This intention involves considering a process of awareness, which is vital to survival and to understanding God's call to women in the ministerial task and in the exercise of their gifts. It also involves considering a rereading of the Bible where women's stories are recovered and their importance as part of the experience of the culture in which they live. However, it also involves understanding Pentecostal women as 'living communities' (who understand God from their femininity, their faith, their feelings, and emotions within their own cultures), which requires listening to and interpreting their voices.[3] It also requires an analysis of the pneumatological understanding of the Pentecostal church in the present so that women with God's call to lead and administer, as gifts received from the Holy Spirit, can exercise their callings without impediments imposed by ecclesiastical structures.

Consequently, we have called this theology of the Hispanic Pentecostal woman a *Pentecostalista* theology. This term refers to an understanding of God from the perspective of Hispanic Pentecostal women. It is a way of naming the reflection that results from women in leadership who strive in the Pentecostal church and specifically in the cultural context of Spanish-speaking churches. It is Pentecostal because it defines the voices of women who have had a profound experience with the Holy Spirit that propels them toward fulfilling God's mission.

For Bernardo Campos, *Pentecostality* 'is a generic name with universal value that refers to the universal experience of all Christians with the Holy Spirit from the Christian experience of Pentecost when the Church of the New Testament was formed'.[4] Conversely, it also identifies other extensions or historizations of that primal experience as *Pentecostalisms*. The theologian well clarifies that Pentecostality is not an exclusive identity of Pentecostals and that it can be defined as the principle and religious practice, informed by the event of Pentecost. It is a universal experience that elevates to the category

---

[3] The phrase 'listen to their voices' is no accident. Epistemologically, it can be said that it is original to the American feminist Carol Gilligan who wrote the book *In a Different Voice*, where she develops a psychology of moral development that contradicts the theory of Lawrence Kohlberg. When Gilligan uses the phrase, she uses it to say that 'when she heard Kohlberg's theory in the voice of women, she heard from them something different from what Kohlberg postulated about moral development in women'. Ultimately, that is what this researcher proposes; that women's voices when heard speak of something other than what the church wants to impose on them and talk about how they experience God and his calling even though the IDDMB in particular and the COG in general make biblical arguments for the denial of third-level credentials for women.

[4] Bernardo Campos, 'Que es la Pentecostalidad?' http://pentecostali dad.com/index.php/2015/10/29/que-es-la-pentecostalidad-2/   October 29, 2015.

of 'principle'. The Pentecostal practices that seek to be histor-ical concretions of that primordial experience.[5]

There is no attempt here to undermine Campos' achieve-ment of bringing the concept of Pentecostality to a universal level. However, I recognize that I use the *Pentecostalista* concept in a particular way, in this case, to name Spanish-speaking Pen-tecostal women, but that, conversely, it is inclusive enough for other voices to find expression to describe, ask, and reflect on the challenge that women pose in the exercise of their gifts within our particular Pentecostal denominations and other de-nominations in general.

---

[5] Campos, 'Que es la Pentecostalidad?' Cf. Bernardo Campos, 'Aspectos Fundamentales de la Teologia Pentecostal', *Hechos: Una Perspectiva Pneumato-lógica* 1.1 (Jan 2019), p. 29.

2

THEOLOGICAL APPROACHES TO THE CONFLICT: PRACTICAL PASTORAL THEOLOGY AND THEOLOGY OF WOMEN

> … but there is a strong conviction abroad
> in the movement today that the era
> of male dominance is fading.
> Harvey Cox[1]

Practical Pastoral Theology

Practical Pastoral Theology (PPT) is understood as that discipline that relates to all fields of pastoral care and the healing of souls, as well as to the introduction into the tasks of building and directing the community and its members and groups.[2] Three traditions prevail in the discipline of the PPT: Ibero-American European theology, Latin American theology, and American theology, each with its various interests. In addition, there are other emerging traditions. For example, the Ibero-American European tradition emerged in 1912 with the Spanish theologian Casiano Floristán. In this tradition the

---

[1] Cox, *Fire from Heaven,* p. 138.
[2] Javier Calvo Guinda, 'Teología Pastoral/ Teología Práctica', in Casiano Floristán (ed.), *Nuevo Diccionario de Pastoral* (Diccionarios San Pablo; Madrid, Spain: San Pablo, 2002), pp. 1462-77.

subjects are the ecclesial pastoral caregivers: the clergy, the magisterium, and the ordained laity. The object is the Church. The methodology that distinguishes this tradition is known as seeing, judging, and acting. For Floristan, the PPT is the actions of the Church and Christians. These actions produce theological reflection. It is an invitation to reflection and then to action, which must in some way embody the practice of Jesus.

However, Latin American Practical Pastoral Theology has the theologian as the subject and the 'comunidades de base' (base communities) as the object. Its methodology is contextual and has been related to Latin American liberationist movements.

Then there is the American tradition. Anton Boisen, who by 1930 begins with the practice of clinical pastoral education or CPE, is identified here at Worcester Psychiatric Hospital, Massachusetts. The subject in this tradition is the theologian and the object of it is the human being and one's experiences in culture. This theology is nourished by the correlate method that emerged from 1924 with Paul Tillich. For Tillich, the theologian's questions emanate from the very existence of the human being. In turn, the Christian message responds with the theology based on the Bible and the Christian tradition. This correlation can happen in reverse, but the important thing is the dynamic question-answer-question. As we have already said, in this model the object of theology is the person themself, whom Boisen calls as the *living human document.* Therefore, what develops is known as *Boisen's case study method,* which is a correlating one since it integrates theology, knowledge of psychology, sociology, and social work, thus creating a hermeneutic model aimed at listening to and knowing in depth the person's experiences of suffering.

Finally, in terms of emerging pastoral theology traditions, there are others such as Asian, Native American, and Caribbean. The following can be said about the latter: it is a tradition that emerges from the Inter-American University of Puerto Rico to the different cardinal points of our land. It is a

PPT where the subject is ecclesial pastoral care with a hybrid methodology: postcolonial and transdisciplinary macroecumenic.[3] This emerging tradition includes notable scholars Jesús Rodríguez,[4] Héctor López Sierra,[5] and Rafael Hiraldo.[6]

Therefore, PPT extends from the daily work or the healing of souls to the context of universities in dialogue with various disciplines, until reaching the hospital, prison, and health care institutions to this day. The PPT continues to transform in order to be relevant to human beings in need of dignity, understanding, liberation, and salvation. In other words, the tasks of the PPT represent the Shalom of God approaching humanity.

Women's or Feminist Theology

In defining feminist theology, we must begin with feminism, which is an ideology and a set of social, political, cultural, and economic movements that aim at equal rights for both men and women. To this end, the feminist movement created a broad set of social theories that gave rise to the emergence of various disciplines. Feminism is attributed to social achievements of transcendental importance such as the female vote. Ana de Miguel presented a historical tour of the feminist movement that divides its manifestation into three periods: premodern feminism, modern feminism, and finally contemporary feminism. Thus, feminism has managed to

---

[3] Readers can become familiar with this concept through the reading of Jesús Rodríguez Sánchez, 'The Emerging Field of Pastoral Theology in Puerto Rico', *The Ecumenical Review* 59.2-3 (February 25, 2007), pp. 221-34.

[4] Sánchez, 'The Emerging Field of Pastoral Theology in Puerto Rico'.

[5] Héctor López Sierra, *Arte Social Crítico, Sentido y Preocupación Ultima* (San Juan, PR: Tamarind Hill Press, 2005), and *Teorías Organizacionales y Dinámicas Religioso-Eclesiales: Acercamiento Transdisciplinario* (San Juan, PR: Ediciones SITUM, 2006).

[6] Rafael Hiraldo, 'Hacia un marco Teórico de la Violencia Domestica desde la Teología Pastoral Práctica: Una aplicación de la Función Correctiva de la Teología Pastoral Protestante en Puero Rico' (PhD, Universidad Interamericana de PR, 2007).

identify truly feminist concerns (where there is awareness of inequality and feminists acted to provoke change) as early as in the enlightenment period in the 18th century, to the radical and liberal feminisms of the 1960s and 1970s and up to their latest trends[7]. As a category of theology, it is worth mentioning that, epistemologically[8] speaking, feminist theology is nourished by the theologies of Latin American liberationism, whose repercussions continue to this day. More precisely, the feminist theology of Latin America that draws on daily experiences (contextual theology) ensures that it seeks the following:

> First, to know life through personal experiences and through the human and social sciences. Then, to interpret these experiences in the light of the Bible ... and understanding that the Spirit can reveal what it means to us today. Third, to try to give a name to women's experiences in a patriarchal society so that we can redeem the past, transform the present, and prepare for tomorrow.[9]

Now, what does the concept of 'feminist theology' mean here? It means doing theology from the perspective of women in their contexts and considering their experiences. It is to construct theology from the hermeneutical privilege of the oppressed (in this case of women), who can conceive of another reality different from the dominant hierarchical and patriarchal paradigm. It is to try to understand the Christian experience from the context of women in general and Pentecostal women in particular.

---

[7] Ana de Miguel Álvarez, 'Feminismos', in Esperanza Bautista, *10 palabras clave sobre violencia de género* (Estella, Navarra: Editorial Verbo Divino, 2004), pp. 217-55.

[8] Epistemology is the science that searches for the nature or origin of human knowledge in its real principles and real functions, the types or kinds of knowledge and methods that can lead to its correct realization in each case.

[9] Ana María Tepedino, 'Feminist Theology as the Fruit of Passion and Compassion', in Virginia Fabella and Mercy Amba Oduyoye (eds.), *With Passion and Compassion: Third World Women Doing Theology* (Maryknoll: NY, Orbis Books, 1988), p. 166.

Historically, the first feminist theologies emerged from the voices of white women in the West and from the Roman Catholic tradition. Little by little, however, other theological expressions were born from women in various contexts. Thus, at last, the voices of women who had been silent in the development of theology continued to be heard. The interesting thing is that we have found in the voice of the *Mujerista*[10] theologians and the Womanists[11] of the United States, answers relevant to our questions.

Protestant theologian Pamela Dickey Young can help us understand the conflict of Pentecostal women. She has explained that the challenge of feminist theology consists of two steps. The first is the stage of criticism, where awareness of oppression is created, all existing literature is documented, and explanation for oppression and exclusion is also explored. The second stage is reconstruction, which means that women's stories are rescued, and doctrines are rebuilt in the light of new critical reflection. From then on, documentation and reconstruction move in parallel, and they continue in the light of new discoveries.[12]

From Feminist Theology to a *Pentecostalista* Theology: Breaking Up and New Theological Links

So, we can recognize that from classical feminist social theories[13] a movement has been generated that has placed us

---

[10] *Mujerista* refers to the theology of Hispanic catholic women in United States. It was developed by the theologian Ada María Isasi-Díaz.

[11] Womanist refers to the theology of Afro-American women in United States. In our case we have studied this theology through the writings of Delores Williams.

[12] Pamela Dickey Young, *Feminist Theology/Christian Theology: In Search of a Method* (Minneapolis, MN: Augsburg Fortress, 1990), pp. 15-17.

[13] We have already mentioned that feminism is attributed to social achievements of transcendental importance such as the women's vote, protection against sexual harassment, equality before the law, and reproductive rights. It should also be noted that feminism is composed of very diverse currents, so some understand that it is more correct to speak of 'feminisms' than of 'feminism' in the singular. Among the wide variety

today in the face of new currents of feminist theologies. As stated above, I would argue that that feminist theologies are not only the daughters of feminist theories, but also of the theologies of liberation. Just as the first-generation theologies of the liberation proclaiming the preferential option for the poor (understood as an economic category) were transformed to include not only the economically poor but the marginalized, the dispossessed, and in the end all those suffering from inequality, so also a new category has emerged in feminist theologies. No doubt, feminist theologies are no longer what they originally were. These new theologies of women of the present time can be identified as emerging or contemporary feminist theologies. These theologies are sketched by women from other cultural contexts from the Majority World, referring to people who have been neglected and who lack the power to shape their future. The term 'Majority World' describes a relationship marked in the past by 'strength and mediated by colonial ties',[14] and I add, postcolonial.

As Puerto Rican women, it is possible that the pastors of the Pentecostal denomination can be located in this emerging paradigm. The struggle of these women and the theological reflection that arises from them reflect a unique identity. This identity is the result of an amalgam of colonial and postcolonial ecclesial and cultural impositions that strengthen oppression and marginalization. It is from there that the

---

of trends that we can find, it is worth mentioning, for example, cultural feminism, liberal feminism, radical feminism, and ecofeminism among others. According to Maggie Humm and Rebecca Walker, the history of feminism can be classified into three waves: the first wave would appear in the late 19th and early 20th centuries and focused mostly on the achievement of women's suffrage; the second wave appears in the 1960s and 1970s and focuses on the liberation of women; finally, the third wave, begins in the 1990s and extends to the present day. See Rebecca Walker, *To Be Real: Telling the Truth and Changing the Face of Feminism* (New York: Anchor Books, 1995), and Maggie Humm, *The Dictionary of Feminist Theory* (Columbus: Ohio State University Press, 1990), p. 278.

[14] Virginia Fabella and R.S. Sugirtharajah, *Diccionario de teologías del Tercer Mundo* (Estella: Editorial Verbo Divino, 2003), p. 380.

pastors of the Pentecostal church also make and understand theology, even if they are not so aware of it. But what are the theological and methodological differences between the *Pentecostalista* theology proposal and the Christian feminist theologies mentioned?

Theological and methodological ruptures

Within emerging feminist theologies, Pentecostal academic women have managed to open up a space for academic reflection that considers their contextual situation. In this regard they speak of their own experiences of marginalization and the possibilities of liberation that will produce justice and peace. Examples of this are the voices of Pentecostal women such as Agustina Luvis and Raquel Echevarria (Puerto Rican), Kimberly Ervin Alexander, Cheryl Bridges Johns, and Estrelda Alexander (Americans), and the voice of this author. In addition, the voices of the women in our research includes those who, although not from the academy, are living human documents and primary resources of our quest for a solution to the conflict.[15]

However, for the purposes of this text, I recognize an epistemological rupture with classical feminism, especially radical feminism. The reasoning here is that from the Pentecostal perspective in general and that of this author in particular, both men and women belong on the same level when it comes to human value and dignity. In this regard, like Dickey Young, we seek to establish theoretical arguments based on a method of theological reflection that recognizes the value both of man and woman in fulfilling the mission of the church.

Similarly, I understand that there is an epistemological rupture with revolutionary feminist theology, because a culture

---

[15] Those interviewed in our research were Puerto Rican women pastors from the Mission Board Church of God. They all had long ministerial and pastoral careers. They have held leading positions in the denomination, even if it is not supposed to be that way. They recounted their difficulties and discrimination on the part of their male brethren in pastoral care and in their churches.

focused on women is not proposed here; rather, the focus is on the value of all human beings. Hence, in using our Pentecostal theology, what is longed for is to re-establish a theological dialogue that can transform the church in particular and society at large. In contrast to the most radical feminist postulates, I believe that although God became incarnated in the male Jesus, he can be the Savior of women also. By accepting him as Savior, women are instilled with hope by the Holy Spirit so that they can take hold of the prophet Joel's promise and therefore be empowered by the Spirit to fulfill their mission as believers who ultimately form Christ's church.

The prophet Joel (2.28) asserts that God would give his Spirit to all; both women and men would prophesy. Furthermore, taking the example of Jesus as recorded in the Gospel of Luke (4.18-19) as the paradigm for Christian ministry means that the Spirit of God is upon all believers, empowering them to give good news to the poor, bring freedom to the oppressed, open their eyes of the blind, and rescue the abused. This is the Good News that the church proclaims about God's salvation; and in this announcement, we are all invited to collaborate.

Furthermore, the perspective of *Pentecostalista* theology seeks to promote the unity of the body of Christ, just as the Apostle Paul presents it when he uses that image of the body to point out that all the members are distinct but form one body. We also recognize here the anthropological, theological principle that all human beings were created in the image of God. Finally, understood from the Pentecostal tradition, it is essential to review the doctrine of the charismata. The Holy Spirit distributes gifts as he wants and to whom he wants for the building up of this same body (1 Cor. 12.12-31). In the words of Agustina Luvis, 'unity is the product of the presence of gifts of the Spirit in the Church'.[16]

---

[16] Agustina Luvis Núñez, 'Sewing a New Cloth: A Proposal for a Pentecostal Ecclesiology Fashioned as a Community Gifted by the Spirit with the Marks of the Church from a Latina Perspective' (PhD diss., Lutheran School of Theology, 2009), p. 77.

Our theological, Pentecostal, and Hispanic path seeks not to exalt the superiority of one gender over the other (which is what machismo does) but we seek equality and the possibility that the relationships between men and women of the Pentecostal church (which serves as a model for other churches) are reciprocal. That is, we are looking for the transformation of relationships. It is a theology that seeks to promote the appreciation of women within the Pentecostal ecclesial context and within the Hispanic cultural context.

New links

What aspects of feminist theory in general and Christian feminism in the particular are binding on the development of a *Pentecostalista* theology? This emerging theological method attempts to unmask patriarchalism in continuity with Christian feminist theologies. First, we utilize vocabulary that reveals patriarchal systems, a vocabulary that must become known in the Pentecostal church, so that the church can become aware of (and develop an understanding of) the situation of inequality and oppression of its women pastors. On the one hand, it identifies the **androcentrism** that is the ideology that legitimizes patriarchy by affirming the idea that the masculine is the norm that governs all that is human and undergirds the systems and practices of social inequalities between men and women.[17]

On the other hand, it should be emphasized that **gender**, as understood within feminist theology and with the help of social sciences and anthropology, is a social construct that varies depending on time or time and place or country. While gender is a social construct, sex is the biological term. Gender is a social construct that creates stereotypes; what is expected of every man and woman in time and space. These stereotypes are perpetuated in every society. Androcentrism does not recognize that gender stereotypes are unfair constructs to the detriment of women. It has been a commitment of feminist theologies to denounce the violence and injustices that such

---

[17] Fabella and Sugirtharajah, *Diccionario de Teologías*, p. 239.

constructs have meant to women. Androcentrism constructs a system where the male is the model and the standard for defining humanity. The male is central, and the rule is that females are excluded from participation at the essential level. However, in trying to understand this concept, we do not agree that gender can be chosen by each individual according to how that person feels. We affirm here that we are born male or female, but we also affirm that even the tradition of the church has insisted on assigning roles to people according to their gender, which translate into oppression and that do not even match the Word of God.[18]

For its part, **sexism** is another ideology that supports patriarchy and is defined as 'the supremacy of man, the superiority of man, and the whole belief system that supports and sustains the aforementioned concept'.[19] In other words, it is the belief that one sex (male) is superior to the other. In many cases these social attitudes and constructions have been the fermenting germ of **misogyny** or hatred of women that culminates in violence against women and more tragically even femicide.

It is a reality that the church has sacralized patriarchy by interpreting some biblical accounts and by using literal interpretation of certain texts. Some of these biblical passages are used constantly to silence women and to prevent them

---

[18] The church has long used certain biblical passages to keep women marginalized. The biblical passages where Jesus interacts with women have not been revised, nor have Paul's writings favoring them from the perspective of trying to resolve the conflict expressed here and in light of new discoveries and tools for biblical interpretation. The narratives of the resurrection where Jesus appears to women have not been taken as hard evidence. In addition, in the classic passages of 1 Corinthians 11 and 1 Timothy 2, only some matters related to women are validated while others are ignored, take the veil, for example or that the woman will be 'saved in childbearing' (1 Tim. 2.15; quotations of Scripture are taken from the New King James Version unless identified otherwise); nor do those verses concerning males apply in these pericopes. Rather, the government of the church has been modeled after an image taken from marriage in Ephesians 5.

[19] Gerda Lerner, *The Creation of Patriarchy* (New York, NY: Oxford University Press, 1986), p. 240.

from acquiring power. The historical facts of our denomination, as well as our culture, have also supported such a position of oppression (marginalization and exploitation). A theology of *Pentecostalista* women in pastoral ministry will affirm that the patriarchal system is not the will of God and is the product of the entry of sin into the world (as reflected in the Garden of Eden narrative). It is then stated that such a sin affects the relationships between men and women in the community of faith that responds to God's call and has a negative impact on the fulfillment of the Church's mission.

Secondly, other binding positions belong, epistemologically speaking, to the order of feminist theologians in general. According to Elisabeth Schüssler Fiorenza, if we want to have the appropriate responses for the marginalization or exclusion of women in the church, we must consider the hermeneutics of experience, domination, social location, suspicion, remembrance, critical assessment, and contextualization.[20] She has raised awareness of the need for a feminist reading of the Bible. Reading the Bible in this way will allow biblical accounts of women who are excluded or who stand on the sidelines or who are represented prejudicially to be rescued. Reading the Bible with women's eyes will supply hopeful answers to women in their struggles and experiences. Following this line of thought, Dickey Young invites everyone to raise awareness of oppression, to document all existing literature, and to seek explanation for oppression and exclusion. Then, after reading the text through the eyes of women, we have to act by means of reconstruction.[21] Both authors point to the rescue of women's stories and to the reconstruction of doctrines in the light of new critical reflection and new discoveries that illuminate biblical accounts.

From the perspective of *Mujerista* theology (of Hispanic Catholic women in the United States) it is also vital to raise

---

[20] Elizabeth Schüssler Fiorenza, *Los caminos de la sabiduría: Una introducción a la interpretación feminista de la Biblia* (Maliaño: Sal Terrae, 2004), pp. 219-49.

[21] Dickey Young, *Feminist Theology/Christian Theology*, pp. 15-17.

awareness of the oppressive structures that dominate their lives. This theology calls for changing these oppressive structures. This theology attempts to mark the sin of structures as a reality that does not allow the revelation of God and his presence to manifest itself in the midst of communities. The second task of this theology is to insist that the life of each believer must find direction by defining a pathway for future growth and development. There is a call here to internalize that a radical change in structures is prevailing, but that will not happen unless a radical change is taken in each of these women. In theological terms this requires repentance, conversion, and reconstruction.[22]

Likewise, from the theology of African-American women such as Delores Williams, it must be recognized that women face multiple barriers within the church. Williams states 'that there is a horrible side to the experience of black women that has to do with sexist oppression at the leadership level and at other levels of Church life'.[23] For African-American women, the Bible as the word of God has to be reinterpreted in a way that provides information about tradition. It is then important to respond to this tradition in daily life. This issue is difficult and complex.

In conclusion, I would prefer to align myself with Dickey Young's approach. She stresses the importance of maintaining the balance between fundamental Christian postulates and the interest of feminists in finding a theology that takes seriously the experience of women and that recognizes equality between men and women.[24]

Where, then, does the selection of these postulates taken from Christian feminist theologies lead? From our perspective, it leads to the development of the constituent elements of *Pentecostalista* theology. Here then, the hermeneutical method and

---

[22] Ada María Isasi-Díaz, *En La lucha/In the Struggle: A Hispanic Women's Liberation Theology* (Minneapolis: Fortress Press, 1993), pp. 17-23

[23] Delores S. Williams, *Sisters in the Wilderness: The Challenge of Womanist God-Talk* (Maryknoll, NY: Orbis Books, 1993), p. 11.

[24] Dickey Young, *Feminist Theology/Christian Theology*, p. 104.

the theological model to be followed are defined as the set of procedures to be considered to express a congruent theological thought system that can do justice to Pentecostal women in general and to Hispanic Pentecostal women of the Church of God in particular. The aim is that we, as a Christian community, can more clearly and intentionally reflect the values of the Kingdom of God in our contexts. The method is both deductive and inductive because the conclusions start from the concrete facts but also from abstract principles and previous ideas. This theological method can be used to address the following audiences: first, the women of IDDMB, then the women of the Church of God and the other Pentecostal women.

Towards a New Paradigm

In the last two decades I have served within the Pentecostal tradition and specifically on the Church of God Mission Board. This is an organization of some openness within Pentecostalism, but it was where I really discovered the other reality, different from that of my childhood and youth. In this denomination women's voices are often silent. Leadership opportunities at the highest hierarchical level are scarce. As an observer and participant in the church, I began a process of reconscience (awareness of oppression or inequality) as proposed by Ada María Isasi-Díaz as one of the first steps towards freedom and equality.[25]

The Pentecostal church has the challenge of integrating women into the fulfillment of the mission. It is said of integration that it is the consequence of the participation of all in all areas of society. To do this, many must receive support from others, which leads to integration into a dynamic process that should include the participation of all members and should be based on equality, not charity.[26]

---

[25] Isasi-Díaz, *En la lucha,* pp. 164-66.
[26] Gómez, Rosa Aparicio, '¿Qué Es Eso Que Llamamos Integración?' *Tiempo de Paz* 76 (2005), pp. 37–47.

As a Pentecostal community it is important that this dialogue highlights the Pentecostal experience, which affirms the dynamic action of the Holy Spirit in the midst of life's experiences. Pentecostals have shown the whole world that the Holy Spirit is empowerment for the mission. It is an experience that I know as a Pentecostal by being part of this ecclesial community and by studying its history. This is the story that Pentecostals identify in Scripture, especially in the Acts of the Apostles, and which is undoubtedly observed throughout the history of the church. This story of what the Pentecostal experience means can also be heard from the voices that Walter Hollenweger records in his book *Pentecostalism.*[27] Similarly, the testimony and experience of founding people, such as Agnes Ozman, Charles Parham, and William Seymour, among many related to the Azusa Street movement in Los Angeles, to the liberating Pentecostal experiences of today, affirm the dynamic action between the divinity and the daily life of the human being.

This dynamic experience of the Holy Spirit, who acts in the midst of the community, levels all believers and makes them all equal. So, it is not possible for the Pentecostal church to turn its back on the Holy Spirit or to ignore the Holy Spirit, even if the church has been institutionalized or has accommodated to culture or has operated with a patriarchal hierarchy. It should be noted that patriarchy is accompanied by privileges and operates through subjugation. Feminist theology has revealed that patriarchy means the manifestation and institutionalization of male dominance over women and the extension of this dominance in society at large. Patriarchy implies that males possess power in all the important institutions of society and that in turn women are prevented from access to such power. However, it does not mean that women are totally devoid of power or rights, influence or resources.[28]

---

[27] Walter Hollenweger, *Pentecostalism: Origins and Developments Worldwide* (Peabody, MA: Hendrickson Publishers, 1997).

[28] Lerner, *The Creation of Patriarchy*, p. 239.

Our reflection and action have allowed for an experience of reconscience. It is this experience that drives us to look with new eyes at the conflict we are dealing with here. Where do we place ourselves as scholars of a conflict that occurs within our own tradition of faith? Beyond a confessional and systematic theology it will be imperative, and indeed very useful, to be placed within a pastoral theology that understands Pentecostal women as living documents[29] or as living human communities; as communities that move, exist, and survive within a broader culture. It is from the platform of Christian feminist pastoral theology that we try to understand the situation of women in the ministry of the church. Once again, Dickey Young's academic work charts a viable route for us. I am in agreement with her that it is necessary to 'open spaces of diverse dialogues where the experience of women is considered in such a way that they can develop to the fullest of their potential, in complete humanity and complementarity with the male gender'.[30]

However, in our struggle, I appreciate the Protestant theologian Letty Russell, who does not want to leave or abandon her Christian tradition because it still shows with its symbols, liturgy, cult, actions (and within the Pentecostal experience through the Holy Spirit) that religious experience

---

[29] The expression is by Anton T. Boisen and arises as an integral part of his case study method. The method of case study did not begin with Anton Boisen but had already begun at Harvard Law School. However, Boisen became familiar with the method while studying with George Albert Coe at Union Theological Seminary in New York. Living human documents were the patients and clients with whom Boisen worked. Boisen said that it was more useful to study the person in his environment and understand it not from the texts of the academy but from what they lived and expressed including their motives, emotions, and religious experiences. Students of pastoral theology who are preparing in the classroom can learn from these living documents. Glenn H. Asquith, Jr, 'The Case Study Method of Anton T. Boisen', *The Journal of Pastoral Care* 34.2 (June, 1980), pp. 84-94.

[30] Dickey Young, *Feminist Theology/Christian Theology*, p. 104.

remains transformative and liberating.[31] Other women have chosen to abandon their ecclesial traditions because of the oppression and exclusion to which they have been exposed. In fact, Russell says that what needs to be done is to analyze what 'we are and do'[32] and try to review it. This invitation from the theologian urges women to be catalyst agents.

However, in this new paradigm I cannot agree with Mary Daly, the first modern female philosopher, who says that Jesus cannot be the Savior and that he cannot serve as a model for women, because 'his masculinity only gives legitimacy to the superiority of the male gender over the female'.[33] Rather, we agree with another feminist theologian, Clara Bingemer, who argues that Christology remains good news of salvation for women who understand that they can work together with men in complementarity so that both reach their full potential.[34] In addition, I agree with Rosemary Radford Ruether, who in *Sexism and God Talk* states that the 'patriarchal style has been to the detriment of both men and women because it has not allowed them (either) to develop to the fullest of their potential'.[35]

---

[31] Letty Russell, *Human liberation in a Feminist Perspective: A Theology* (Philadelphia, PA: Westminster, 1974), and *The Future of Partnership* (Philadelphia, PA: Westminster, 1979).

[32] Russell, *Human liberation in a Feminist Perspective*, p. 184.

[33] Mary Daly, *Beyond God the Father: Toward a Philosophy of Women's Liberation* (Boston, Massachusetts: Beacon Press, 1973), pp. 71-72.

[34] Clara Bingemer, 'Mujer y Cristología: Jesucristo y la Salvación de la Mujer', in María Pilar Aquino (ed.), *Aportes para una Teología desde la mujer* (Madrid: Ediciones Biblia y Fe, 1988), p. 93.

[35] Rosemary Radford Ruether, *Sexism and God Talk: Toward a Feminist Theology* (Boston, Massachusetts: Beacon Press, 1983), p. 116.

3

PENTECOSTAL PNEUMATOLOGY

Pentecostal Pneumatology: How Pentecostals Understand the Holy Spirit

In its most basic definition, pneumatology is the study of the person and work of the Holy Spirit. It is clear from careful study of the Bible that the Holy Spirit possesses personality; he is an active and divine person. The Holy Spirit is part of the divine Trinity. The Old Testament implies this Trinitarian relationship, and the New Testament confirms it. Through Scripture the Holy Spirit is represented by symbols such as wind, breath, water, fire, oil, dove, and seal. The work of the Holy Spirit began before Pentecost, for he was a divine agent in creation, was the author of the Scriptures, and was active in the life and ministry of Jesus (see Gen. 1.2, 26, Lk. 4.1, and 2 Pet. 1.21). According to Wesleyan theology, the Holy Spirit is the administrator of the divine plan of salvation under the new covenant.[1] Jesus taught about the Holy Spirit by declaring that the Spirit was present in and with believers, that the Spirit is the paraclete, and that Jesus would baptize with the Holy Spirit.

---

[1] Charles W. Carter, R. Duane Thompson, and Charles R. Wilson (eds.), *A Contemporary Wesleyan Theology: Biblical, Systematic, and Practical* (Salem, Ohio: Schmul Publishing Co., 1992), I, pp. 425-27.

It is relevant to understand that the Holy Spirit is the Father's promise to the believers of the first century. That this promise is still in force today is fundamental to the Pentecostal experience in particular and for Christianity in general. The revival that occurred in the early twentieth century is the result of believing and reaffirming that Pentecost's experience in the book of Acts was still in force and vital to the church's mission to go all over the world and proclaim that the Kingdom of God had come close. The church is established by the Holy Spirit and according to 1 Corinthians, the Holy Spirit distributes gifts to the church as he chooses (1 Cor. 12.11). These gifts are gifts of grace (*charismata*). They are the divinely ordained means and faculties with which Christ enables his church to fulfill his task. The gifts of the Holy Spirit are supernatural capacities for service and are determined by the character of the ministry to be made. They are vital to the success of the church mission. These gifts are distributed at the discretion of the Spirit. Not all church members receive the same gifts, and the Bible has at least four different lists of these gifts.[2]

The Pentecostal understanding of the Holy Spirit is based on the doctrine of the Trinity. A God who exists in three persons: God the Father, God the Son, and God the Holy Spirit.[3] The Holy Spirit is Comforter and Teacher, who bears witness to Christ and the Father's promise to every believer. Through the Holy Spirit the believer is freed from sin (sanctification) to live in the Spirit. The community of faith, of which the believer is a part through baptism in water, is conceptualized as the community of the Spirit. The presence of the Holy Spirit in the life of believers produces the fruit of the Spirit in addition to investing them with 'power from on high' for service and to equipping them with spiritual gifts for the building up of the Church.

---

[2] Orton Wiley and Paul T. Culbertson, *Introducción a la Teología Cristiana* (Kansas City, Missouri: Casa Nazarena de Publicaciones, 1992), pp. 275-86.

[3] French L. Arrington, *Christian Doctrine a Pentecostal Perspective* (Cleveland, TN: Pathway Press, 1992), I, p. 127.

For a Pentecostal, the Holy Spirit is manifested in the believer through the spiritual experience of baptism in the Holy Spirit. This experience is subsequent to conversion.[4] The testimony of John the Baptist and the Lucan account of the early church in the book of Acts of the Apostles is the scriptural evidence for this doctrine. Classical Pentecostals add to this doctrine speaking in other languages (*glossolalia*) as initial evidence of baptism in the Holy Spirit.[5]

In practice and in the life of the community of faith the Pentecostal sees the Holy Spirit distributing gifts that translate into different ministries. On the one hand, gifts are given to the Church in general and to the believer in particular by the Spirit in his sovereignty by deciding its distribution. On the other hand, gifts are not just for the benefit of the person to whom they have been given; rather, they are for the edification of the whole church. Likewise, the functionality of gifts is given in the context of the different functions that believers have in the Body of Christ.[6]

Pentecostals (including charismatic and neo-charismatic movements) have impacted many areas of Church life in almost every country in the world with their vitality and fervor, which come precisely from their experiences in the Holy Spirit. Participants in this tradition share an experience of exuberant and vibrant worship, an emphasis on personal religious experience, and the gifts of the Spirit. In addition, they claim miracles, signs, and wonders and heartily proclaim 'life in the Spirit' which allows them to live out God's will daily.

The Holy Spirit, therefore, more than a theological language, is an experience, a life-giving experience. Although there is knowledge of who the Holy Spirit is according to the Holy Trinity, although he is understood as a person and not as a force (even though it gives strength as understood from the Lucan narrative in Acts 1.8), and although Pentecostal

---

[4] Arrington, *Christian Doctrine*, I, p. 51.
[5] Arrington, *Christian Doctrine*, I, p. 64.
[6] Stanley M. Horton (ed.), *Teología Pentecostal: un aperspectiva pentecostal* (Deerfield Beach, FL: Editorial Vida, 1996), p. 466.

theologians[7] have developed a doctrinal language that is understandable to scholars of all ecclesial communities, it is no less true that for Pentecostals the Holy Spirit is revealed by means of personal experience. According to Steven Land, for Pentecostals

> the starting point for understanding God and the world is through the Holy Spirit, who is 'God in Us', and this has theological implications. The presence of the Holy Spirit constitutes the Church. Creeds keep faith, but they cannot limit the sovereignty of the Spirit.[8]

We must return to the question that gives rise to this reflection. How is it that the Holy Spirit is understood from a Pentecostal perspective? Among some vital issues, we can say that the Pentecostal community has taught that the Holy Spirit distributes different gifts to the members of the body for the purpose of building and equipping the church. Pentecostals teach that gifts do not belong to recipients, but rather the Spirit administers them as empowerment for missional service. Moreover, and very relevant to us, Pentecostals believe that the Holy Spirit distributes the gifts as he wants and that all gifts are important, regardless of their manifestations.

The Pentecostal Church understands that just as the body has many members and all are necessary, all believers need each other with the graces bestowed upon each one and that this interdependence is only possible in the bond of love.[9] These graces (*charismata*, from *charis* 'grace') are gifts for believers in Christ. If the Holy Spirit is for all believers, the gifts are also to all and for all. Their purpose is the building up of the body of Christ. In his first epistle, the Apostle Peter exhorts,

---

[7] Guy P. Duffield and Nataniel M. Van Cleave, *Fundamentos de Teología Pentecostal* (San Dimas, California: Life Pacific College, segunda edición, 2002). Arrington, *Christian Doctrine*, I, pp. 127-42.

[8] Pentecostal theologian Steven Land was President of the Pentecostal Theological Seminary of the Church of God in Cleveland, TN. See: *Pentecostal Spirituality: A Passion for Kingdom* (JPTSup 1; Sheffield, UK: Sheffield Academic Press, 1993), p. 34.

[9] See 1 Corinthians 12-13.

As each one has received a gift, minister it to one another, as good stewards of the manifold grace of God. If anyone speaks, let him speak as the oracles of God. If anyone ministers, let him do it as with the ability which God supplies, that in all things God may be glorified through Jesus Christ, to whom belong the glory and the dominion forever and ever. Amen.[10]

The Apostle Paul explains further,

Now you are the body of Christ, and members individually. And God has appointed these in the church: first apostles, second prophets, third teachers, after that miracles, then gifts of healings, helps, administrations, varieties of tongues.[11]

Then in his Epistle to the Romans, Paul mentions that believers have different gifts, according to the grace that has been given to them:

Having then gifts differing according to the grace that is given to us, let us use them: if prophecy, let us prophesy in proportion to our faith; or ministry, let us use it in our ministering; he who teaches, in teaching; he who exhorts, in exhortation; he who gives, with liberality; he who leads, with diligence; he who shows mercy, with cheerfulness.[12]

It is the Holy Spirit who gives gifts of faith, service, teaching, exhortation, generosity, presiding, mercy, prophesying, performing miracles, gifts of tongues, healings, and administering, among others. We recognize that gifts are not limited to a single pericope of the Bible (despite the traditional references to the nine gifts of the Spirit found in 1 Cor. 12.8-10) and that other gifts indeed abound. In fact, what I could postulate is that today the Holy Spirit continues to be creative in giving a great diversity of gifts depending on the cultural

---

[10] 1 Peter 4.10-11.
[11] 1 Corinthians 12.27-28.
[12] Romans 12.6-8.

context and the needs of a community of faith in the place where it proclaims the message of salvation and liberation. In other words, just as the communities are diverse and just as the members of the body are many, in the same way there are many different gifts. This diversity is necessary. This is how it is expressed by the theologian Dario López:

> The pastoral and missionary consequence of the existence of a diversity of spiritual gifts within Christian congregations is the fact that not all believers have the same task within a congregation and that diversity is essential to ensure that there is a healthy church. This requires the members of a church to be responsible for the administration of the gifts they have received and also respectful of the task or commission that their brethren have in the faith, whose gifts are so valuable and necessary for the integral health of the whole community of disciples, inasmuch as the gift that he or she has is due only to God's mercy.[13]

As we reflect on the conflict of women in the Pentecostal church, we discover an inconsistency in the exercise of gifts. This inconsistency is delineated here through the following questions. Why does the Holy Spirit give gifts of healing, for example, to men and women for use in any context (public or private) without causing any conflict? Why does the Holy Spirit give gifts of tongues to both men and women in different contexts without it causing a conflict? Why does the Holy Spirit give gifts of teaching and service to men and women to apply in different contexts without this church seeing any conflict in it? However, when the Holy Spirit gives gifts of governance and administration (where they exercise authority over others) to women, the church manifests tension and looks for reasons to limit the women's exercise of this *charism*? It seems that Pentecostal women can administer in their homes, but not in the church. They may preside in the church, but not

---

[13] López Rodríguez, *La fiesta del Espíritu*, p. 144.

in a committee or executive structure. Are not administrative structures part of the church? Those who lead and administer are expected to do so because they have received God's gift for leading and administering the church. This should hold true for women as well as for men.

Therefore, in our reflection and dialogue with Pentecostal women pastors (with honesty and humility), we proposed this question: Why does the third person of the Trinity give gifts of leadership and administration to women? Why do these women feel 'unworthy' and inside they have to expect to be forgiven for being women and have to pray that they should be given a chance to exercise what God has already given them? Is it possible that the Holy Spirit has erred in giving these gifts to his female vessels? It is an honest question, and the honest answer is 'No! The Holy Spirit of God is not in error'.

As a Pentecostal, I proclaim, I reaffirm, and fight for the church to understand that the Holy Spirit of God has given gifts and the Spirit has not erred. It is the Holy Spirit himself who decides what capacity or gift he will give to each one (1 Cor. 12.11). It can then be concluded that in considering the conflict of women and their ability to exercise their gifts, it is the church that has erred by not allowing them to exercise their gifts and ministries on an equal standing and with the same rights and responsibilities as the men.

Now, human beings are the ones erring. Human interpreters are the ones who have made a mistake. Like the prophet Daniel, the church must recognize its sin. Like the prophet, the church must pray to God and exclaim, 'O Lord, righteousness belongs to You, but to us shame of face … to our kings, our princes, and our fathers, because we have sinned against You' (Dan. 9.7-8). It is the church's duty to recognize, affirm, and validate what the Holy Spirit gives to the community of faith no matter whether the recipient of the gift is male or female. To do any less is sin. Therefore, repentance and action are expected in order to reconstruct our theology.

4

CONSTITUTIVE ELEMENTS OF A *PENTECOSTALISTA* THEOLOGY

Now, what are the theological sources of our model of a *Pentecostalista* theology? Its sources include the very experiences of women and the actions that are called for as a result of reflection. Women's experiences are human experiences that testify of discrimination. Their experiences reflect the struggle to obey God and to exercise the gifts received from the Holy Spirit within a patriarchal system. The women interviewed for this project entered the pastoral ministry in response to a call from God. These women are convinced of this call, and their conviction rests on the following assertions:

- 'The ministry is Divine.' With this they clearly establish that there is a higher force or power, which is not subject to the earthly powers. It does not depend on human will or human decisions. That is, the person (woman) has been separated and chosen for ministry.

- 'God is the one who calls.' It is known with certainty what is the provenance of this call and that by being divine is inescapable. No matter what is left behind, the circumstances of life do not matter. The ministry arises from a deep conviction that answering God's call is the right thing to do.

- 'God has no preferences.' Being the man and woman created in his image and likeness, God makes no distinctions. In Christ, 'there is neither male nor female' (Gal. 3.28). God looks at the heart and places in every heart the task or command to shepherd. One woman pastor remarked, 'God sent Christ to die for humanity and I am there. He calls both women and men.'

- 'This did not come from us but came from God.' When this reality is understood, only then do these women understand why they struggle against circumstances, mindsets, prejudices, but they do not give up. For they are not alone, because this ministry comes with the assurance that can only be bestowed by the Holy Spirit.

It is precisely because they know that they are not alone that they can face their daily struggles. Their ministry is backed by the Paraclete, the power of the Spirit is sufficient to fulfill God's mission in the midst of all dilemmas. In other words, the commitment made by women to a call within the church is an act of love for all humanity. They accept God's call to them, from their femininity, in every sense of the word, even if this involves challenges to their personal lives and to their own faith.

In short, the women pastors of this Pentecostal Church are adamant that their call is from God and that God has no preferences and makes no exceptions. Moreover, they count on the promise of the Holy Spirit as a guarantee that they can carry out God's mission. They understand that the God who calls them is the God who enables them. (This argument has always been used by Pentecostals.) These women are willing to work hard and to sacrifice, even though they do not have equal standing with the men. They are intelligent, determined, courageous women, and they are willing to abandon everything for ministry.

My own reflection is another source from which this methodological model emanates. This reflection has led me to conclude that there is inequality between men and women in this church. Men are privileged while women exist here in a second-class category. This reflection compels action in the interests of making the church fairer and more equitable. So, what are the constituent elements of the proposed theological model? The elements are the task, the hermeneutical method, and the interlocutors.

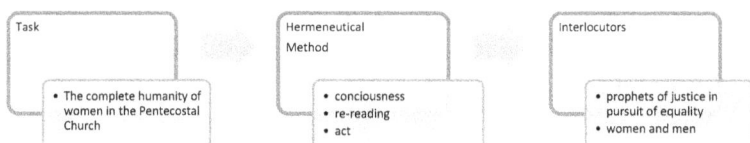

Task	Hermeneutical Method	Interlocutors
• The complete humanity of women in the Pentecostal Church	• conciousness • re-reading • act	• prophets of justice in pursuit of equality • women and men

Figure 1
Constitutive Elements of the *Pentecostalista* Theology model

So we offer this pattern as a way forward, so that we can work as brothers and sisters in resolving the conflict of Pentecostal women with the church. Women pastors seek to have their divine calling validated by their church, and they seek to create a just Church that articulates believers' experiences with the Holy Spirit consistently, whether that believer is a woman or a man. Again, we turn to the disciplines of Practical Pastoral Theology and to the Theologies of Women.

The Task

What should be the task in light of the Practical Pastoral Theology of the Pentecostal woman? The mission is to promote the total and complete humanity of the female human being. It is a matter of ontological equality with the male human being. It is not a question of denigrating the opposite gender but of identifying that both men and women operate in patriarchal structures. It is important to emphasize that both women and men intrinsically carry the image of God in themselves.

From the Pentecostal tradition in particular, it is hoped that everyone will be able to reach 'the measure of the stature of the fulness of Christ' (Eph. 4.12-13) and to affirm with the Apostle Paul that 'there is neither male nor female; for you are all one in Christ Jesus' (Gal. 3.28). In Christ, women and men are equal when they answer God's call. The response to this call, with the obvious result of the exercise of the gifts received by the Holy Spirit, has caused much pain, doubt, and frustration for women. Women are not wandering spirits nor souls in churches, but are embodied in real bodies that feel, suffer, fight, and survive in a secular and ecclesial culture that does not do them justice. This injustice is not tolerable and cannot be accepted any longer. Justice is a vital characteristic of the Kingdom of God; it is a mark of the new people constituted by God.

Women are a living text. Women pastors are the living communities that help to illuminate divinity; and within the theological and pastoral task, it is necessary to discover and show that way of understanding God. It is the function of theologians to interpret how they feel, experience, live, and relate to God. Theologian Leonor Aida Concha, a Catholic nun, says that 'women are subjects of theology and have become protagonists and are forging processes'.[1] Justo L. González and José D. Rodríguez also expressed that women are 'emerging subjects of theology'.[2]

For Delores Williams, reading the Bible from a feminist perspective finds in the story of Hagar, Sarah's servant, another story of the oppressed woman who is used, abused, and rejected. Williams uses the story of Hagar to frame the experience of the African-American woman and her oppression that comes from slavery. This feminist lens privileges women, including those in our churches, as emerging subjects of theology.[3]

---

[1] Concha, Leonor Aida, 'Luchas Y Logros En El Proceso de La Liberación de La Mujer: Análisis Desde México, Centroamérica Y El Caribe', in María Pilar Aquino and Luz Beatriz Arellano (eds.), *Aportes Para Una Teología Desde La Mujer: Colaboraciones de Teólogas Latinoamericanas En La Conferencia Intercontinental de Mujeres Teólogas Del Tercer Mundo* (Nuevo Éxodo 5; Madrid: Escuela Bíblica: Editorial Biblia y Fe, 1988), p. 59.

[2] José David Rodríguez, *Introducción a la Teología* (Méjico: Publicaciones El Faro, 2002), pp. 43-45, and Justo L. González, *Mañana: Christian Theology from a Hispanic Perspective* (Nashville, TN: Abingdon Press, 1990), p. 48.

[3] Williams, *Sisters in the Wilderness*, pp. 15-31.

At the same time, a theology of the Pentecostal woman will have to consider the person of the Holy Spirit and how that theology is informed by the experiences of women, in this case, women's experiences of calling to pastoral ministry within a church that preaches the importance of a life and response of life in the Spirit to carry out the task to which they are all called. This emerging theology will have to bring to light how the Holy Spirit becomes relevant to this gender conflict that seems to diminish the church's missionary call. In addition, we must trust what the Holy Spirit points out and how the Spirit compels women to act in a liberating way.

Finally, as part of the task, let us briefly consider the following question: What are the historical, social, and theological-pastoral foundations that enable women of the denomination to continue to exercise their pastoral ministry in this patriarchally structured church? Some answers may be outlined. Historical reasons include the inescapable fact that women were a vital part of this Pentecostal church in its early days. This church, born because of the dissatisfaction experienced in a well-to-do and institutionalized church, welcomed the women called by God as equals, fulfilling the church's mission. This is not only characteristic of our denomination, but it is also characteristic of the entire Pentecostal movement of the early twentieth century. This diversity and inclusion is no secret to women or even to Pentecostal males.

As for the social biases, consideration should be given to the civil rights movement that was fueled by African-Americans in the United States to combat discrimination. Consideration should also be given to Christian feminist movements, both Catholic and Protestant, in different parts of the world. Both movements affected ecclesial culture. African-Americans had to make their spaces again in denominations, and as time passed there have been reconciliations of some denominations on the issue of race. At the same time, women began studying at universities, thus changing Christian demographics. Each year more women have decided to prepare themselves for God's call and have ceased to be the silent voices of theology. Our Pentecostal church was not excluded from these cultural impacts.

No less important are the theological–pastoral reasons that impel the women of this church towards the exercise of pastoral work even within a patriarchal structure. As a result of this investigation, three reasons can be mentioned. First, Puerto Rican women are active today within the church, that is, from the local church to the national church. This has been the case since the church began in Puerto Rico in 1944. Therefore, in practice women imitate others in the work of the faith community. Second, the Pentecostal pastors of this denomination understand that they received a divine call, that God does not show preference for certain people, and that he calls both men and women. Essentially, after that understanding, who should stop women in their response to God's call for the task, including the tasks of administration and leadership? At the same time, Pentecostals believe, preach, teach, and encourage the imparting of power by the Holy Spirit. The Holy Spirit sanctifies them and empowers them. The Holy Spirit gives the *charismata*. Without a doubt, in considering these reasons, it will have to be concluded that women, within this Pentecostal church, may continue to exercise pastoral ministry even though this church is patriarchal in essence and discriminates against them. However, this form of patriarchy will continue to be painful for everyone in the Pentecostal church and as a result could continue to fragment the denomination and weaken the mission and work of the church.

It is worth noting that this theology arises from the Puerto Rican context, from a small Caribbean archipelago. Therefore, the experiences of Puerto Rican pastors are expressed in indigenous voices, and they do not intend in any way to speak for other women, although others may be able to identify with experiences similar to those of Puerto Rican women.

5

HERMENEUTICAL METHOD: AWARENESS, BIBLICAL REREADING, AND ACTING UNDER THE DIRECTION OF THE HOLY SPIRIT

The Church, the body of Christ, is relevant as she fulfills her mission: 'Go therefore and make disciples of all the nations … teaching them to observe all things that I have commanded you' (Mt. 28.19-20). It is also inherent in the mission of the church to go out and to set captives free under the authority of the Spirit of God (Lk. 4.18-19; Isa. 61.1-2; 42.7; 49.9). Jesus' proclamation that the Kingdom of God was already among us (Lk. 17.21) evokes a behavior of the believer in line with the values of the Kingdom of God. This conduct of the believer and the church must be constantly evaluated to ensure that believers walk the right path and accomplish the task effectively. Fortunately, the PPT allows an approach to ecclesial practice, specifically in the context of IDDMB, so that it is possible to assess through reflection whether what is practiced is consistent with God's calling and purpose for women in the church, and ultimately for the whole church. In Floristan's words, 'theology therefore has a relationship with the building up of the people and with social reality'.[1]

The hermeneutical method of our theological model is defined as the set of procedures that are considered to express the system of thought in such a way that justice can be done for the women of the Pentecostal church. The aim is to make it possible, as a Christian community, to reflect more clearly or more intentionally the values of the Kingdom of God in the church, community, society, and ultimately in the world. The intention is to fulfill the liberating task in an integral way within the community of faith. The method is both inductive and deductive because the conclusions start from the concrete facts but also incorporate abstract principles and previous ideas.[2] For feminist theologies, concrete facts are the everyday, the struggle, the experiences of women in their particular contexts. For pastoral theology it refers to the living human document, to the person who from her own experiences communicates and transmits a message.

Abstract principles and previous ideas of the method refer to postulates of the Pentecostal church, to what it teaches and preaches. On these teachings one can build the method of a *Pentecostalista* theology. These teachings may include the church's understanding of the Holy Spirit and the gifts possessed by the Pentecostal church. Also, these teachings include the idea that all are called, but that it is the responsibility of the human being to respond. Once the human being answers affirmatively to God's call and repents of their sins, then that person becomes part of the community of faith. These redeemed people serve God's purpose to reconcile human beings with God through Jesus Christ. So, this hermeneutic model is postulated from the experiences of the women pastors as concrete facts to the valuable teachings of the church as part of their principles and ideas. As a system at last, the model must progress in an order or set of steps. So,

---

[1] Casiano Floristán, *Teología Práctica: Teoría y Praxis de la Acción Pastoral* (Salamanca: Sígueme, 1991), p. 353.

[2] Floristán, *Teología Práctica*, p. 361.

what are the steps of the methodology of the *Pentecostalista* theological model?

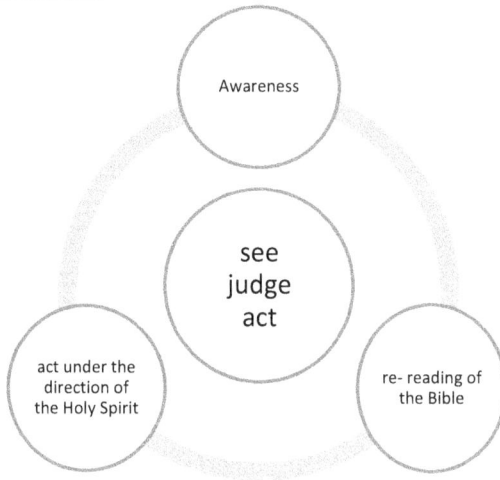

Figura 2
Hermeneutical Process of the *Pentecostalista*. Theology

Awareness

The first step is **awareness.** We must ask, what is going on? Then we must **see.** We must have the ability to observe spontaneously, then in a directed and finally critical way. In the Pentecostal dynamic awareness also includes leaving 'space for the Spirit of God' to act on men and women on a personal level, although the personal level definitely has repercussions on the ecclesial level, on the people of God. In this step, we must also observe the phenomena, structures, theories at stake, and internal mechanisms.[3] By analyzing the conflict of women in the Pentecostal context, it is now possible to ask: Why can't the woman of the COG be part of the structures where decisions are made that affect the whole church at the national and global levels? Why can't they exercise leadership according to the gifts of the Spirit?

---

[3] Floristán, *Teología Práctica*, p. 362.

Women ministers are allowed to pastor, teach, attend a congregation, and in Puerto Rico they are part of the bodies of local counselors;[4] however, they cannot hold other positions in the hierarchy of power. The theories at stake are those of power and dominance concurrent with the patriarchal system. The structure of this church is hierarchical, centralized, patriarchal, and dominated by white males in the Southern United States. However, the biblical arguments for sustaining such dominance are weak and anachronistic. Moreover, in our opinion, they are sinful and require repentance. Also, with regard to the game of power, women must understand that the church's refusal to open leadership spaces for women is due in part because this openness for women is perceived by the men as a partial closing or limiting such spaces for them. As Martin Luther King, Jr astutely observed, 'Lamentably, it is an historical fact that privileged groups seldom give up their privileges voluntarily'.[5]

Finally, internal mechanisms prevent women from continuing to rise to where decisions are made. Mission Board women trained for the task, based on gifts received, cannot obtain the bishop credentials that would allow them to be part of the total decision-making of this church. These women, who responded to God's call, need to find ways to resolve the conflicts that such a situation leads to in their ministries and in their personal lives. Isasi-Díaz has insisted that the Church itself 'is oppressive because it does not provide the spaces for women (Catholics) to find themselves the possibility of developing to the fullest of their capacities, in complementarity with the male gender'. Pentecostal women need to be aware of the fact that they do not have equal standing with male ministers. It is vital for the women of this church to become

---

[4] As explained, this is the most important body of every local church and only at the 2010 world assembly was it approved so that women could belong to it after several years of struggle. However, in public relations women have been part of these bodies since the beginning of the IDDMB in the early 20th century.

[5] Martin Luther King, Jr, 'Letter from Birmingham Jail', *The Christian Century* (June 12, 1963), p. 768.

aware of their own oppression, which for these purposes results in discrimination and subordination and makes it impossible for women to lead and administer at the same level as the male ministers.

Rereading the Bible

The second step in this hermeneutical cycle is the **rereading of the Bible.** Once the awareness of marginalization, oppression, injustice, or inequality is awakened, then we must ask ourselves: What does God reveal to us in such a situation? Answers to this question come through the process of discernment, which I call **judging.** Whatever issue is discovered must then be correlated with the values of the Kingdom in the light of the teachings of God and Jesus. The proposed hermeneutical model of emerging theology invites an encounter with the Word of God to see how the church acts either in agreement with or in dissonance with the Word of God. This process is reading the Bible as a dialogue between friends, and the process is inspired by the Spirit. The process brings questions, circumstances, and needs to the text and through the text to the Lord. It allows God to reveal his own agenda inasmuch as he speaks to readers through his Word.[6] This meeting with God through his Word will have as its main objective a liberating experience and an action towards justice.

As a result of our research, we testify to the inequality that exists between men and women in the church. Nevertheless, patriarchal leaders continue to present arguments favoring the continuation of the present oppressive ecclesial structure. As would be expected, the Bible is often quoted in support of the present system that limits the ministry and leadership (exercising of God's gifts) of women.

Now, what does the Bible mean for Pentecostals? For Pentecostals, the Bible is the Word of God. The

---

[6]Andrew Davies, 'What Does It Mean to Read the Bible as a Pentecostal?', *Journal of Pentecostal Theology* 18 (2009), pp. 221-22.

denomination's Declaration of Faith affirms the belief in the verbal inspiration of the Bible: 'The Church of God accepts the whole Bible, rightly divided. The New Testament is its only rule for government and discipline.'[7] Sometimes the church in the full has come together to interpret the Scriptures and make known the teachings revealed. However, more than a doctrine, the Bible is an experience with the Holy Spirit.

> Pentecostals generally read the Bible not to learn from the history of Israel, from the development of the Christian theology of the first church or of the life of Christ, but to find Christ in the text, and provide an opportunity for the Holy Spirit to speak to our spirit. In our tradition, the reading, interpretation, and proclamation of Scripture has little to do with intellectual comprehension and everything to do with the revelation of the divine God.[8]

I agree with Andrew Davies that 'when Pentecostals bring their shared experiences into the text, they find the assurance they need to support faith with Scripture and have no doubts as to what they see in it'[9] and that Pentecostals 'prefer to interpret Scripture more by encounter than by exegesis ... and simpler, that they can allow the Spirit of God to tell them anything he wants them to know from the words on the page'.[10]

A common approach between feminist theologies and this *Pentecostalista* theology is precisely the importance and approach that will be used when seeking an answer in the Bible. If you want to have the appropriate answers for the marginalization or exclusion of women in the church, you should consider,

---

[7] Declaration no. 1. *Las Enseñanzas, Disciplina y Gobierno de la Iglesia de Dios* (Asamblea 2008), p. 15.

[8] *Las Enseñanzas, Disciplina y Gobierno de la Iglesia de Dios* (Asamblea 2008), p. 16.

[9] *Las Enseñanzas, Disciplina y Gobierno de la Iglesia de Dios* (Asamblea 2008), p. 17.

[10] Davies, 'What Does It Mean to Read the Bible as a Pentecostal?', pp. 220-21.

among others, the hermeneutics of suspicion.[11] The theologian invites female students to read the Bible in this way (with suspicion) because women, in her opinion, have learned to read it from a hermeneutics of respect, acceptance, and obedience. This feminist theologian advocates that a hermeneutics of deconstruction be considered, an approach that is able to analyze linguistic and cultural practices that are in the functioning of the dominant structure, especially among women. When approaching Scripture from this perspective students will then question and criticize the ideas and concepts that hide the deepest truths.[12] Therefore, the biblical accounts can be rescued, that is, the stories of women who are excluded or on the sidelines or presented with prejudice. Reading the Bible with women's eyes will allow us to offer answers to women in their struggles and experiences.

Delores Williams has described the suffering and struggle for the survival of African American women, and she also recognizes the barriers within the church for women.[13] One way these women can survive their experiences is through their appreciation and appropriation of the Bible. Likewise, Pentecostal women consider the Bible as the Word of God. It is a word that inspires and nourishes life. The Bible is a comfort in times of tribulation; it is guidance and direction when wisdom is sought; and it also provides answers to questions and doubts. As for African Americans, the Bible is a force for Pentecostal women. Pentecostal women 'read the Bible not to grab it but for God to grab us through it. And once the Word has impacted our hearts, it becomes fire in our bones.'[14] Just as this Womanist Theologian took the story of Hagar and reinterpreted it for her own sufferings of slavery, Pentecostal women have also seen themselves in the eyes of women such

---

[11] Davies, 'What Does It Mean to Read the Bible as a Pentecostal?', p. 220.

[12] Davies, 'What Does It Mean to Read the Bible as a Pentecostal?', p. 221.

[13] Williams, *Sisters in the Wilderness,* p. 11.

[14] Williams, *Sisters in the Wilderness,* p. 223.

as Mary, Deborah, Ruth, and Esther, among many others. Therefore, the challenge continues to be the patriarchal use of the Bible to continue to support the oppressive structures, because the Bible itself is framed in ancient cultural patterns that include patriarchal structures.

Finally, as a primary issue for feminist theologies, one that is vital to me as a Pentecostal, it is important that we rescue the stories of women from the Bible. We must search for the stories and reinterpret them by stripping them of the patriarchal envelope in which they are ordinarily received.[15] The women pastors of our denomination have already expressed their view that the biblical texts must be revisited and retaught from the perspective of women.

Acting Under the Direction of the Holy Spirit

The third step in the method is **to act under the direction of the Holy Spirit.** In this hermeneutical model we are in a position to answer the question: What should be done? The answer, of course is to **act.** Here theology is militant and committed and, at the same time, leads to transformative

---

[15] For example, you could take the story of the girl and the Syrian general Naaman found in 2 Kings 5. This pericope is usually understood to highlight that God used this girl to encourage her master's faith and to go to Samaria to seek healing through the prophet. But how many times did anyone wonder what this experience of being kidnapped and taken to another nation as a slave meant? This adolescent girl was a victim of oppression and slavery. It is possible to find God accompanying this girl in her life tragedy and that God was her strength in the midst of the crisis. It is possible to present the comforting God, the God who suffers for injustices and who rewards the dispossessed with the strength of his power and his presence. In any case, in studying a story like this, the suffering of an oppressed person should not be overlooked. Another example to highlight is the narration of the hunched woman of Luke's gospel whom Jesus calls Abraham's daughter. In doing so, Jesus places her on the same level as the male sons of Abraham, so the promises are also for women. However, the women (especially Mary Magdalene) to whom the message of the resurrection was given, are examples that must necessarily be reread with the eyes of a woman, in such a way that their value for the liberation of all is highlighted.

action.[16] Isasi-Díaz's feminist voice theology aspires first to raise awareness of the woman's situation so that she is able to act. She explains that as soon as Hispanic women in the United States understand their situation, starting from their religious experience that they embrace, they begin to fight for their dignity and the values that give them identity.[17] Floristan expresses that at this stage of action, sinful structures must be classified.[18] In regard to sinful structures, Eldin Villafañe argues that when the church[19] excludes, marginalizes, persecutes, oppresses, and uses its structure to criminalize women, it operates in a sinful framework.[20]

This action requires work. It is a backbone issue and will require a change of thinking. Pentecostals generally understand that when there are difficult or delicate situations 'it is best to pray'. However, although I value my spiritual tradition of prayer, it is no less true that I also understand that sometimes while praying and after praying you must move forward to action. Certainly, Pentecostal women who are conscientious of their oppression and then encounter the biblical readings that free them from their captivity, must move to do justice on behalf of one another. The dynamic power of the Spirit cannot be confined to momentary and personal experiences but it must encourage its vessels to witness freedom in Christ throughout their environment. The church must be the place of both personal and social transformation. In this regard, Villafañe expresses himself eloquently:

> The charismatic empowerment of the Spirit has received a unique and distinctive emphasis in Pentecostalism. Pentecostals ... tended to interpret this experience in a

---

[16] Floristán, *Teología Práctica*, p. 364.

[17] Isasi-Díaz, *En la Lucha*, p. 161.

[18] Floristán, *Teología Práctica*, p. 364.

[19] Here we refer to the Church in its broadest sense and throughout its entire history.

[20] Eldin Villafañe, *El Espíritu liberador: Hacia una ética social pentecostal hispanoamericana* (Buenos Aires; Grand Rapids, MI: Eerdmans, 1996), pp. 152-54.

limited way. While it is true that Pentecostalism has been recognized as a powerful force in evangelization, world missions, the growth of the church and spirituality, it is equally true that its services and prophetic voices against sinful social structures and for social justice have been absent.[21]

So, how have we acted in relation to the conflict of the women pastors of the Pentecostal denomination? It should be mentioned that for several years (last four international assemblies of the COG) the issue of women's ordination has been discussed. Each international assembly once again confronted the ecclesiological culture and questioned its hermeneutics. Speeches both in favor and against the ordination of women were presented by different segments of the church. Again, it is very difficult for the male bishops to accept what women do and to legitimize it. However, among the laity in the local churches, the ministry and authority of women continues to be accepted.

A group of women and men of the IDDMB filed a motion at the ministerial (business) meeting in January 2005. This motion stated that Puerto Rican women ministers who held the second level of credentials (ordained minister) would be eligible to occupy all leadership positions in the ecclesial structure with the exception of National Bishop. The measure was unanimously approved. Interestingly, in other Latin American countries women are also being elected to the bodies of national advisors. In addition, here in PR, women are appointed as district supervisors and as members of some boards of directors, such as those of the Theological University, the Retirement Plan, and the Board of Trustees of the denomination. These are concrete actions that have been taken after the raising of awareness and after re-examination of biblical passages that validate the total participation of women in the affairs of the Kingdom of God and its church.

---

[21] Villafañe, *El Espíritu Liberador*, p. 174.

6

INTERLOCUTORS: PENTECOSTAL WOMEN AND MEN TOGETHER AS PROPHETS OF JUSTICE

The Church represents Christ on earth; and, according to Scripture, believers are Christ's ambassadors (2 Cor. 5.20). The Kingdom of God is not only eschatological since its values can already be practiced from the present time. Nevertheless, this Kingdom is different from earthly kingdoms. This was the refrain of the Lord Jesus during his earthly ministry. The Kingdom of God must be characterized by justice and peace. For the peace of God, which is a fruit of his Spirit, to be abundant in the church, justice is necessary. In the midst of injustice, peace can not abound.

The Old Testament prophets confronted God's people and the surrounding peoples about sin and injustice. The prophets interpreted the times, denounced injustice, and called on the people to approach God in the context of ethical behavior, while extending mercy and justice to others. The prophets recognized that it was necessary to change attitudes and respond to God's call.

Similarly, Jesus preached that his Kingdom was not structured as the earthly Kingdoms. Although men occupied the highest echelons of power in Jerusalem, it was to women that Jesus chose first to deliver his message of the resurrection.

Christ's church is called to show the world an image of Christ, of the Father, and of the Holy Spirit that makes no distinction between race, color, ethnicity, age, stage of life, social class, or gender. I would argue, in contrast to early COG leader A.J. Tomlinson, that the church is not a government. The church is not an American democratic-style government, nor is it even a government compared to the earthly ones. It is therefore incorrect to continue to teach that women have no role in the governing affairs of the church in which they serve. This does not do women justice and does not produce peace.

What we must have today are new interpreters of the Word of God, new prophets who, recognizing the authority of this Word, enact righteousness in the body of Christ and demonstrate equality in the Kingdom of God. These new prophets are the men and women who, led by the Holy Spirit, overcome the church's historical decisions that were detrimental to women. They are men and women who recognize that God gives spiritual gifts to all for the building up of the body and that gender does not disqualify them from exercising the gifts, including gifts of leadership and administration. These prophets of justice are men and women, who, in the light of the new approaches to biblical interpretation, can minister in an up-to-date and effective way to a society that demands equity and equality for the ministry and leadership of Pentecostal women. The Pentecostal church must no longer fight against the Holy Spirit who summons women to fulfill the mission. Once again, I point to 1 Pet. 4.10-11:

> As each one has received a gift, minister it to one another, as good stewards of the manifold grace of God. If anyone speaks, let him speak as the oracles of God. If anyone ministers, let him do it as with the ability which God supplies, that in all things God may be glorified through Jesus Christ, to whom belong the glory and the dominion forever and ever. Amen.

The Holy Spirit gives gifts to people for the upbuilding or edification of the church. Then the church itself affirms, recognizes, and validates what the Holy Spirit delivers. This is affirmed by the Apostle Paul in Rom. 12.6-8 and 1 Cor. 12.27-28:

> Having then gifts differing according to the grace that is given to us, let us use them: if prophecy, let us prophesy in proportion to our faith; or ministry, let us use it in our ministering; he who teaches, in teaching; he who exhorts, in exhortation; he who gives, with liberality; he who leads, with diligence; he who shows mercy, with cheerfulness.

> Now you are the body of Christ, and members individually. And God has appointed these in the church: first apostles, second prophets, third teachers, after that miracles, then gifts of healings, helps, administrations, varieties of tongues.

7

CONCLUSION: CALL TO THE ALTAR

In conclusion, the proposed *Pentecostalista* theological model is presented from the author's ecclesial context in Pentecostalism and from her cultural context of Puerto Rico. It emerges from the action that results as a product of reflection. It has as its source the experiences of Pentecostal women, particularly of the pastors of the IDDMB. Its standard refers to the pneumatological Christian doctrine of the Pentecostal church. Its goal is to free women ministers of IDDMB from all discrimination and inequality in cooperation with the men of this church until we build a more just church for generations to come. This is vitally important so that the message of salvation for all is intellectually credible and consonant in practice with the values of the Kingdom of God and with the practices and teachings of Jesus.

We propose a theological and biblical model so that the experience of God's call to Pentecostal women can be acknowledged by Pentecostal men with the intention that we both be one body in fulfilling God's mission. The model is built from an emerging and contemporary feminist perspective. The proposed model contains the following constituent elements: the task, a hermeneutical method, and the partners.

First, the task is to promote the total and complete humanity of the female human being in equality with the male human being. As a hermeneutical method it has been proposed first, a process of awareness – which is vital to the survival and the understanding God's call for women in the ministerial task.

Secondly, the model demands a rereading of the Bible in which women's stories are recovered and valued as part of the contemporary ecclesiastical culture. For Pentecostals, reading the Bible is essential, inasmuch as we have explained that the Bible is regarded as the Word of God for all circumstances. Pentecostals appropriate the Word of God in order to survive the circumstances of life. Pentecostals believe,

> Every part of Scripture is God-breathed and useful one way or another – showing us truth, exposing our rebellion, correcting our mistakes, training us to live God's way. Through the Word we are put together and shaped up for the tasks God has for us (2 Tim. 3.16-17, *The Message Bible*).

Finally, the model requires that the church (both male and female) act under the direction of the Spirit so that they can build a more just community of faith. Under the direction of the Spirit, this Pentecostal church needs to be stripped of oppressive structures. It will be necessary for the American church to regard congregations outside its territory as equal and uncolonized. The church must show openness to share power not only with women, but also with other races. This will enable a more effective fulfillment of the church's mission.

Thus, arise the interlocutors or prophets of justice. These are the new interpreters of the Word of God, new prophets who enact righteousness in the body of Christ and demonstrate the Kingdom of God today. We understand that the new prophets are the men and women who, led by the Holy Spirit, overcome the church's historical decisions that have been detrimental to women. It must be a commitment of Pentecostal theology to denounce injustices and inequalities and social negative formulations such as sexism, androcentrism, and misogyny. Men and women are needed who can recognize that God gives spiritual gifts to all believers.

The ethnographic nature of this research[1] was the vehicle to understand the worldview of some of the Pentecostal, Puerto Rican women pastors giving us the opportunity to understand their struggles and conflicts, but also their strength and courage. It is clear from the investigation that Pentecostal women pastors struggle with their call and try to validate it, which is possible with the help of the Holy Spirit. However, they suffer much pain and injustice in the process.

It is possible that the women pastors of the IDDMB will continue to exercise their pastoral ministry within the patriarchal structure of the church, as to this day; but if so, this will lead to increasingly intense tensions that may result in the deterioration of the church. The church will be effective only when it affirms that all believers are recipients of the Holy Spirit and that both men and women receive gifts as the Spirit wills and for the building up of the body of Christ. The church must reconsider its positions in such a way that they do justice to the ministry of women in all areas of the church, including its administration.

I conclude that the development of a new non-patriarchal, non-sexist structure – a structure intrinsically tied to the values of the Kingdom of God of equality, justice, and equity – is necessary. The model of the Hispanic Pentecostal woman confirms that the patriarchal structure is not the will of God but is the product of sin. This sin affects relations between men and women within pastoral ministry because it places them in inequality of conditions.

It is then relevant to state that in developing a *Pentecostalista* theology, I do not intend to exalt the superiority of a gender, which is what machismo does; rather, I propose an ecclesiology of equity that makes possible reciprocal relationships between men and women of the Pentecostal church. That is, this model proposes the transformation of relationships. It is a theology that seeks to promote the appreciation of women within

---

[1] Ethnography is an investigation method which allows the investigator to interact with the different social groups in order to know what they think and what they feel. In other words, it is an investigative tool.

the Pentecostal ecclesial context and within the Hispanic cultural context.

Charles W. Conn, a historian of the COG, writes, 'Christianity has survived by exhibiting an ability to judge itself with candor, to correct itself sincerely, to strengthen itself with humility, and to advance its cause in the face of chaos'.[2] Sometimes, says Conn, 'you must direct efforts to save people to save yourself', referring to the church.[3] The power of the Holy Spirit understood by the apostles and the early Christian communities remains in force in Pentecostal theology. The experience with the Holy Spirit is how Pentecostal pastors validate their call to ministry and can take courageous positions even in the face of discrimination and subordination. The Holy Spirit is liberating.

This concern for the integration of women into the full ministry should not detract from the Pentecostal church. I propose that the same duties, responsibilities, and privileges be recognized to both men and women in the church. God and his Holy Spirit have already called and trained both men and women; so, let the church reaffirm and validate what has already been good to the Holy Spirit:

> I beseech you therefore, brethren, by the mercies of God, that you present your bodies a living sacrifice, holy, acceptable to God, which is your reasonable service. And do not be conformed to this world, but be transformed by the renewing of your mind, that you may prove what is that good and acceptable and perfect will of God (Rom. 12.1).

We concur with Charles Conn, in 'that the victory of one will be the victory of all and that the strengthening of one will be the strengthening of all'.[4]

So, God help us!

---

[2] Charles W. Conn, *Como ejército poderoso: La historia de la Iglesia de Dios 1886-1976* (trans. Wilfredo Estrada Adorno; Cleveland, TN: Editorial Evangélica, 1995), p. 155.

[3] Conn, *Como ejército poderoso*, p. 180.

[4] Conn, *Como ejército poderoso*, p. 331.

BIBLIOGRAPHY

Arrington, French L., *Christian Doctrine: A Pentecostal Perspective* (3 vols.; Cleveland, TN: Pathway, 1992).

Asquith, Glenn H. Jr, 'The Case Study Method of Anton T. Boisen', *The Journal of Pastoral Care* 34.2 (June, 1980), pp. 84-94.

Bautista, Esperanza, *10 Palabras Clave Sobre la Violencia de Género* (Estella: Verbo Divino, 2004).

Bingemer, Clara, 'Mujer Y Cristología: Jesucristo Y La Salvación de La Mujer', in María Pilar Aquino and Luz Beatriz Arellano (eds.), *Aportes Para Una Teología Desde La Mujer: Colaboraciones de Teólogas Latinoamericanas En La Conferencia Intercontinental de Mujeres Teólogas Del Tercer Mundo* (Nuevo Éxodo 5; Madrid: Escuela Bíblica: Editorial Biblia y Fe, 1988).

Campos, Bernardo, 'Qué Es La Pentecostalidad?'; Accessed October 29, 2015; http://pentecostalidad.com/index.php/2015/10/29/que-es-la-pentecostalidad-2/.

Carter, Charles W., R. Duane Thompson, and Charles R. Wilson (eds.), *A Contemporary Wesleyan Theology: Biblical, Systematic, and Practical* (Grand Rapids, MI: Francis Asbury Press, 1983).

Concha, Leonor Aida, 'Luchas Y Logros En El Proceso de La Liberación de La Mujer: Análisis Desde México, Centroamérica Y El Caribe', in María Pilar Aquino and Luz Beatriz Arellano (eds.), *Aportes Para Una Teología Desde La Mujer: Colaboraciones de Teólogas Latinoamericanas En La Conferencia Intercontinental de Mujeres Teólogas Del Tercer Mundo* (Nuevo Éxodo 5; Madrid: Escuela Bíblica: Editorial Biblia y Fe, 1988).

Conn, Charles W., 'Como ejército poderoso: La historia de la Iglesia de Dios 1886-1976' (trans. Wilfredo Estrada Adorno; Cleveland, TN: Editorial Evangélica, 1995).

Cox, Harvey, *Fire from Heaven: The Rise of Pentecostal Spirituality and the Reshaping of Religion in the Twenty-First Century* (Cambridge, MA: Da Capo Press, 2001).

Daly, Mary, *Beyond God the Father: Toward a Philosophy of Women's Liberation* (Boston: Beacon Press, 1973).

Davies, Andrew, 'What Does It Mean to Read the Bible as a Pentecostal?', *Journal of Pentecostal Theology* 18.2 (September, 2009), pp. 216–29.

Dickey Young, Pamela, *Feminist theology/Christian Theology: In Search of Method* (Minneapolis: Fortress Press, 1990).

Duffield, Guy P., and Nathaniel M. Van Cleave, *Fundamentos de Teología Pentecostal* (Bogotá, Colombia: Editorial Buena Semilla, 2nd edn; 2002).

Enseñanzas, Disciplina Y Gobierno de La Iglesia de Dios, 72 Asamblea General Internacional 2008 (Cleveland, TN: Editorial Evangélica, 2009).

Fabella, Virginia, and R.S. Sugirtharajah, *Diccionario de teologías del Tercer Mundo* (Estella: Editorial Verbo Divino, 2003).

Floristán, Casiano, *Teología Práctica: Teoría y Praxis de la Acción Pastoral* (Salamanca: Sígueme, 1991).

Gilligan, Carol, *In a Different Voice: Psychological Theory and Women's Development* (Cambridge, MA: Harvard University Press, 1993).

Gómez, Rosa Aparicio, '¿Qué Es Eso Que Llamamos Integración?' *Tiempo de Paz* 76 (2005), pp. 37–47.

González, Justo L., *Mañana: Christian Theology from a Hispanic Perspective* (Nashville: Abingdon Press, 1990).

Hiraldo Román, Rafael, 'Hacia Un Marco Teórico de La Violencia Domestica Desde La Teología Pastoral Práctica: Una Aplicación de La Función Correctiva de La Teología Pastoral Protestante En Puerto Rico' (PhD diss., Universidad Interamericana de PR, 2007).

Horton, Stanley M. (ed.), *Teología Sistemática: Una Perspectiva Pentecostal* (Deerfield, FL: Editorial Vida, 1996).

Hollenweger, Walter J., *Pentecostalism: Origins and Developments Worldwide* (Peabody, MA: Hendrickson Publishers, 1997).

Humm, Maggie, *The Dictionary of Feminist Theory* (Columbus: The Ohio State University Press, 1990).

Isasi-Díaz, Ada María, *En La lucha/In the Struggle: A Hispanic Women's Liberation Theology* (Minneapolis: Fortress Press, 1993).

Land, Steven J., *Pentecostal Spirituality: A Passion for the Kingdom* (JPTSup 1; Sheffield, UK: Sheffield Academic Press, 1993).

Lerner, Gerda, *The Creation of Patriarchy* (New York: Oxford University Press, 1986).

López Rodríguez, Darío, *La fiesta del espíritu: espiritualidad y celebración pentecostal* (Lima: Puma, 2006).

López Sierra, Héctor, *Arte social crítico, sentido y preocupación última: Reflexiones teóricas y metodológicas alternativas sobre ciencias humanas e interpretación del fenómeno religioso-cultural en la sociedad global contemporánea* (Caguas, PR: Tamarind Hill Press, 2005).

—*Teorías organizacionales y dinámicas religioso-eclesiales: acercamiento transdisciplinario* (Hato Rey, PR: Publicaciones Puertorriqueñas, 2006).

Luvis Núñez, Agustina, 'Sewing a New Cloth: A Proposal for a Pentecostal Ecclesiology Fashioned as a Community Gifted by the Spirit with the Marks of the Church from a Latina Perspective' (PhD diss., Lutheran School of Theology, 2009).

Nuevo diccionario de pastoral (Madrid, España: San Pablo, 2002).

Rodríguez, José David, *Introducción a la teológia* (México, DF: El Faro, S.A. de C.V., 2002).

Ruether, Rosemary Radford, *Sexism and God-Talk: Toward a Feminist Theology* (Boston: Beacon Press, 1983).

Russell, Letty M., *Human Liberation in a Feminist Perspective: A Theology* (Philadelphia: Westminster Press, 1974).

—*The Future of Partnership* (Philadelphia: Westminster Press, 1979).

Sánchez, Jesús Rodríguez, 'The Emerging Field of Pastoral Theology in Puerto Rico', *The Ecumenical Review* 59.2–3 (April 7, 2007), pp. 221–34.

Schüssler Fiorenza, Elisabeth, *Los caminos de la sabiduría: Una introducción a la interpretación feminista de la Biblia* (Maliaño: Sal Terrae, 2004).

Tepedino, Ana María, 'Feminist Theology as the Fruit of Passion and Compassion', in Virginia Fabella and Mercy Amba Oduyoye (eds.), *With Passion and Compassion: Third World Women Doing Theology: Reflections from the Women's Commission of the Ecumenical Association of Third World Theologians* (Maryknoll, NY: Orbis Books, 1988).

Villafañe, Eldin, *El Espíritu liberador: Hacia una ética social pentecostal hispanoamericana* (Buenos Aires; Grand Rapids, MI: Eerdmans, 1996).

Walker, Rebecca, *To Be Real: Telling the Truth and Changing the Face of Feminism* (New York: Anchor Books, 1995).

Wiley, H. Orton, and Paul T. Culbertson, *Introducción al la teología cristiana* (Kansas City, MO: Beacon Hill Press, 1948).

Williams, Delores S., *Sisters in the Wilderness: The Challenge of Womanist God-Talk* (Maryknoll, NY: Orbis Books, 1993).

Index of Biblical References

Index of Authors

www.ingramcontent.com/pod-product-compliance
Lightning Source LLC
Chambersburg PA
CBHW070010100426
42741CB00012B/3181